Percy Byssl

by

John Addington Symonds

The Echo Library 2006

Published by

The Echo Library

Echo Library
131 High St.
Teddington
Middlesex TW11 8HH

www.echo-library.com

Please report serious faults in the text to complaints@echo-library.com

ISBN 1-40680-899-7

CONTENTS

LIST OF AUTHORITIES

1 THE Poetical and Prose Works of Percy Bysshe Shelley, edited by Mrs. Shelley. Moxon, 1840, 1845. 1 volume.
2 The Poetical Works, edited by Harry Buxton Forman. Reeves and Turner, 1876-7. 4 volumes.
3 The Works of Percy Bysshe Shelley, edited by W.M. Rossetti. Moxon, 1870. 2 volumes.
4 Hogg's Life of Shelley. Moxon, 1858. 2 volumes.
5 Trelawny's Records of Shelley, Byron, and the Author. Pickering, 1878. 2 volumes.
6 Shelley Memorials, edited by Lady Shelley. Smith and Elder. 1 volume.
7 Medwin's Life of Shelley. Newby, 1847. 2 volumes.
8 Shelley's Early Life, by D.F. McCarthy. Chatto and Windus. 1 volume.
9 Leigh Hunt's Autobiography. Smith and Elder.
10 W.M. Rossetti's Life of Shelley, included in the edition above cited, Number 3.
11 Shelley, a Critical Biography, by G.B. Smith. David Douglas, 1877.
12 Relics of Shelley, edited by Richard Garnett. Moxon, 1862.
13 Peacock's Articles on Shelley in "Fraser's Magazine," 1858 and 1860.
14 Shelley in Pall Mall, by R. Garnett, in "Macmillan's Magazine," June, 1860.
15 Shelley's Last Days, by R. Garnett, in the "Fortnightly Review," June, 1878.
16 Two Lectures on Shelley, by W.M. Rossetti, in the "University Magazine," February and March, 1878.

CHAPTER 1

BIRTH AND CHILDHOOD

IT is worse than useless to deplore the irremediable; yet no man, probably, has failed to mourn the fate of mighty poets, whose dawning gave the promise of a glorious day, but who passed from earth while yet the light that shone in them was crescent. That the world should know Marlowe and Giorgione, Raphael and Mozart, only by the products of their early manhood, is indeed a cause for lamentation, when we remember what the long lives of a Bach and Titian, a Michelangelo and Goethe, held in reserve for their maturity and age. It is of no use to persuade ourselves, as some have done, that we possess the best work of men untimely slain. Had Sophocles been cut off in his prime, before the composition of "Oedipus"; had Handel never merged the fame of his forgotten operas in the immortal music of his oratorios; had Milton been known only by the poems of his youth, we might with equal plausibility have laid that flattering unction to our heart. And yet how shallow would have been our optimism, how fallacious our attempt at consolation. There is no denying the fact that when a young Marcellus is shown by fate for one brief moment, and withdrawn before his springtime has bought forth the fruits of summer, we must bow in silence to the law of waste that rules inscrutably in nature.

Such reflections are forced upon us by the lives of three great English poets of this century. Byron died when he was thirty-six, Keats when he was twenty-five, and Shelley when he was on the point of completing his thirtieth year. Of the three, Keats enjoyed the briefest space for the development of his extraordinary powers. His achievement, perfect as it is in some poetic qualities, remains so immature and incomplete that no conjecture can be hazarded about his future. Byron lived longer, and produced more than his brother poets. Yet he was extinguished when his genius was still ascendant, when his "swift and fair creations" were issuing like worlds from an archangel's hands. In his case we have perhaps only to deplore the loss of masterpieces that might have equalled, but could scarcely have surpassed, what we possess. Shelley's early death is more to be regretted. Unlike Keats and Byron, he died by a mere accident. His faculties were far more complex, and his aims were more ambitious than theirs. He therefore needed length of years for their co-ordination; and if a fuller life had been allotted him, we have the certainty that from the discords of his youth he would have wrought a clear and lucid harmony.

These sentences form a somewhat gloomy prelude to a biography. Yet the student of Shelley's life, the sincere admirer of his genius, is almost forced to strike a solemn key-note at the outset. We are not concerned with one whose "little world of man" for good or ill was perfected, but with one whose growth was interrupted just before the synthesis of which his powers were capable had been accomplished.

August 4, 1792, is one of the most memorable dates in the history of

English literature. On this day Percy Bysshe Shelley was born at Field Place, near Horsham, in the county of Sussex. His father, named Timothy, was the eldest son of Bysshe Shelley, Esquire, of Goring Castle, in the same county. The Shelley family could boast of great antiquity and considerable wealth. Without reckoning earlier and semi-legendary honours, it may here be recorded that it is distinguished in the elder branch by one baronetcy dating from 1611, and by a second in the younger dating from 1806. In the latter year the poet's grandfather received this honour through the influence of his friend the Duke of Norfolk. Mr. Timothy Shelley was born in the year 1753, and in 1791 he married Elizabeth, daughter of Charles Pilford, Esquire, a lady of great beauty, and endowed with fair intellectual ability, though not of a literary temperament. The first child of this marriage was the poet, named Bysshe in compliment to his grandfather, the then living head of the family, and Percy because of some remote connexion with the ducal house of Northumberland. Four daughters, Elizabeth, Mary, Hellen, and Margaret, and one son, John, who died in the year 1866, were the subsequent issue of Mr. Timothy Shelley's marriage. In the year 1815, upon the death of his father, he succeeded to the baronetcy, which passed, after his own death, to his grandson, the present Sir Percy Florence Shelley, as the poet's only surviving son.

Before quitting, once and for all, the arid region of genealogy, it may be worth mentioning that Sir Bysshe Shelley by his second marriage with Miss Elizabeth Jane Sydney Perry, heiress of Penshurst, became the father of five children, the eldest son of whom assumed the name of Shelley-Sidney, received a baronetcy, and left a son, Philip Charles Sidney, who was created Lord De l'Isle and Dudley. Such details are not without a certain value, inasmuch as they prove that the poet, who won for his ancient and honourable house a fame far more illustrious than titles can confer, was sprung from a man of no small personal force and worldly greatness. Sir Bysshe Shelley owed his position in society, the wealth he accumulated, and the honours he transmitted to two families, wholly and entirely to his own exertions. Though he bore a name already distinguished in the annals of the English landed gentry, he had to make his own fortune under conditions of some difficulty. He was born in North America, and began life, it is said, as a quack doctor. There is also a legend of his having made a first marriage with a person of obscure birth in America. Yet such was the charm of his address, the beauty of his person, the dignity of his bearing, and the vigour of his will, that he succeeded in winning the hands and fortunes of two English heiresses; and, having begun the world with nothing, he left it at the age of seventy-four, bequeathing 300,000 pounds in the English Funds, together with estates worth 20,000 pounds a year to his descendents.

Percy Bysshe Shelley was therefore born in the purple of the English squirearchy; but never assuredly did the old tale of the swan hatched with the hen's brood of ducklings receive a more emphatic illustration than in this case. Gifted with the untameable individuality of genius, and bent on piercing to the very truth beneath all shams and fictions woven by society and ancient usage, he was driven by the circumstances of his birth and his surroundings into an exaggerated warfare with the world's opinion. His too frequent tirades against:—

> The Queen of Slaves,
> The hood-winked Angel of the blind and dead,
> Custom,—

owed much of their asperity to the early influences brought to bear upon him by relatives who prized their position in society, their wealth, and the observance of conventional decencies, above all other things.

Mr. Timothy Shelley was in no sense of the word a bad man; but he was everything which the poet's father ought not to have been. As member for the borough of Shoreham, he voted blindly with his party; and that party looked to nothing beyond the interests of the gentry and the pleasure of the Duke of Norfolk. His philosophy was limited to a superficial imitation of Lord Chesterfield, whose style he pretended to affect in his familiar correspondence, though his letters show that he lacked the rudiments alike of logic and of grammar. His religious opinions might be summed up in Clough's epigram:—

> At church on Sunday to attend
> Will serve to keep the world your friend.

His morality in like manner was purely conventional, as may be gathered from his telling his eldest son that he would never pardon a mesalliance, but would provide for as many illegitimate children as he chose to have. For the rest, he appears to have been a fairly good landlord, and a not unkind father, sociable and hospitable, somewhat vain and occasionally odd in manner, but qualified for passing muster with the country gentlemen around him. In the capacity to understand a nature which deviated from the ordinary type so remarkably as Shelley's, he was utterly deficient; and perhaps we ought to regard it as his misfortune that fate made him the father of a man who was among the greatest portents of originality and unconventionality that this century has seen. Toward an ordinary English youth, ready to sow his wild oats at college, and willing to settle at the proper age and take his place upon the bench of magistrates, Sir Timothy Shelley would have shown himself an indulgent father; and it must be conceded by the poet's biographer that if Percy Bysshe had but displayed tact and consideration on his side, many of the misfortunes which signalized his relations to his father would have been avoided.

Shelley passed his childhood at Field Place, and when he was about six years old began to be taught, together with his sisters, by Mr. Edwards, a clergyman who lived at Warnham. What is recorded of these early years we owe to the invaluable communications of his sister Hellen. The difference of age between her and her brother Bysshe obliges us to refer her recollections to a somewhat later period—probably to the holidays he spent away from Sion House and Eton. Still, since they introduce us to the domestic life of his then loved home, it may be proper to make quotations from them in this place. Miss Shelley tells us her brother "would frequently come to the nursery, and was full of a peculiar kind of pranks. One piece of mischief, for which he was rebuked, was running a stick through the ceiling of a low passage to find some new chamber, which could be made effective for some flights of his vivid imagination." He was very much attached to his sisters, and used to entertain them with stories, in which "an alchemist, old and grey, with a long beard," who was supposed to abide mysteriously in the garret of Field Place, played a prominent part. "Another favourite theme was the 'Great Tortoise,' that lived in Warnham Pond; and any unwonted noise was accounted for by the presence of this great beast, which was made into the fanciful proportions most adapted to excite awe and wonder." To his friend Hogg, in after-years, Shelley often spoke about another reptile, no mere creature of myth or fable, the "Old Snake," who had inhabited the gardens of Field Place for several generations. This venerable serpent was accidentally killed by the gardener's scythe; but he lived long in the poet's memory, and it may reasonably be conjectured that Shelley's peculiar sympathy for snakes was due to the dim recollection of his childhood's favourite. Some of the games he invented to please his sisters were grotesque, and some both perilous and terrifying. "We dressed ourselves in strange costumes to personate spirits or fiends, and Bysshe would take a fire-stove and fill it with some inflammable liquid, and carry it flaming into the kitchen and to the back door." Shelley often took his sisters for long country rambles over hedge and fence, carrying them when the difficulties of the ground or their fatigue required it. At this time "his figure was slight and beautiful,—his hands were models, and his feet are treading the earth again in one of his race; his eyes too have descended in their wild fixed beauty to the same person. As a child, I have heard that his skin was like snow, and bright ringlets covered his head." Here is a little picture which brings the boy vividly before our eyes: "Bysshe ordered clothes according to his own fancy at Eton, and the beautifully fitting silk pantaloons, as he stood as almost all men and boys do, with their coat-tails near the fire, excited my silent though excessive admiration."

When he was ten years of age, Shelley went to school at Sion house, Brentford, an academy kept by Dr. Greenlaw, and frequented by the sons of London tradesmen, who proved but uncongenial companions to his gentle spirit. It is fortunate for posterity that one of his biographers, his second cousin Captain Medwin, was his schoolfellow at Sion House; for to his recollections we owe some details of great value. Medwin tells us that Shelley learned the classic languages almost by intuition, while he seemed to be spending his time in dreaming, now watching the clouds as they sailed across the school-room window, and now scribbling sketches of fir-trees and cedars in memory of Field Place. At this time he was subject to sleep-walking, and, if we may credit this biographer, he often lost himself in reveries not far removed from trance. His favourite amusement was novel-reading; and to the many "blue books" from the Minerva press devoured by him in his boyhood, we may ascribe the style and tone of his first compositions. For physical sports he showed no inclination. "He passed among his school-fellows as a strange and unsocial being; for when a holiday relieved us from our tasks, and the other boys were engaged in such sports as the narrow limits of our prison-court allowed, Shelley, who entered into none of them, would pace backwards and forwards—I think I see him now—along the southern wall, indulging in various vague and undefined ideas, the chaotic elements, if I may say so, of what afterwards produced so beautiful a world."

Two of Shelley's most important biographical compositions undoubtedly refer to this period of his boyhood. The first is the passage in the Prelude to "Laon and Cythna" which describes his suffering among the unsympathetic inmates of a school:—

> Thoughts of great deeds were mine, dear Friend, when first
> The clouds which wrap this world from youth did pass.
> I do remember well the hour which burst
> My spirit's sleep: a fresh May-dawn it was,
> When I walked forth upon the glittering grass,
> And wept, I knew not why; until there rose
> From the near school-room, voices, that, alas!
> Were but one echo from a world of woes—
> The harsh and grating strife of tyrants and of foes.
>
> And then I clasped my hands and looked around—
> —But none was near to mock my streaming eyes,
> Which poured their warm drops on the sunny ground—
> So without shame I spake:—"I will be wise,
> And just, and free, and mild, if in me lies
> Such power, for I grow weary to behold
> The selfish and the strong still tyrannize
> Without reproach or check." I then controlled
> My tears, my heart grew calm, and I was meek and bold.
>
> And from that hour did I with earnest thought
> Heap knowledge from forbidden mines of lore,
> Yet nothing that my tyrants knew or taught
> I cared to learn, but from that secret store
> Wrought linked armour for my soul, before
> It might walk forth to war among mankind.
> Thus power and hope were strengthened more and more
> Within me, till there came upon my mind
> A sense of loneliness, a thirst with which I pined.

The second is a fragment on friendship preserved by Hogg. After defining that kind of passionate attachment which often precedes love in fervent natures, he proceeds: "I remember forming an attachment of this kind at school. I cannot recall to my memory the precise epoch at which this took pace; but I imagine it must have been at the age of eleven or twelve. The object of these sentiments was a boy about my own age, of a character eminently generous, brave, and gentle; and the elements of human feeling seemed to have been, from his birth, genially compounded within him. There was a delicacy and a simplicity in his manners, inexpressibly attractive. It has never been my fortune to meet with him since my school-boy days; but either I confound my present recollections with the delusions of past feelings, or he is now a source of honour and utility to every one around him. The tones of his voice were so soft and winning, that every word pierced into my heart; and their pathos was so deep, that in listening to him the tears have involuntarily gushed from my eyes. Such was the being for whom I first experienced the sacred sentiments of friendship." How profound was the impression made on his imagination and his feelings by this early friendship, may again be gathered from a passage in his note upon the antique group of Bacchus and Ampelus at Florence. "Look, the figures are walking with a sauntering and idle pace, and talking to each other as they walk, as you may have seen a younger and an elder boy at school, walking in some grassy spot of the play-ground with that tender friendship for each other which the age inspires."

These extracts prove beyond all question that the first contact with the outer world called into activity two of Shelley's strongest moral qualities—his hatred of tyranny and brutal force in any form, and his profound sentiment of friendship. The admiring love of women, which marked him no less strongly, and which made him second only to Shakespere in the sympathetic delineation of a noble feminine ideal, had been already developed by his deep affection for his mother and sisters. It is said that he could not receive a letter from them without manifest joy.

"Shelley," says Medwin, "was at this time tall for his age, slightly and delicately built, and rather narrow-chested, with a complexion fair and ruddy, a face rather long than oval. His features, not regularly handsome, were set off by a profusion of silky brown hair, that curled naturally. The expression of his countenance was one of exceeding sweetness and innocence. His blue eyes were very large and prominent. They were at times, when he was abstracted, as he often was in contemplation, dull, and as it were, insensible to external objects; at others they flashed with the fire of intelligence. His voice was soft and low, but broken in its tones,—when anything much interested him, harsh and immodulated; and this peculiarity he never lost. He was naturally calm, but when he heard of or read of some flagrant act of injustice, oppression, or cruelty, then indeed the sharpest marks of horror and indignation were visible in his countenance."

Such as the child was, we shall find the man to have remained unaltered through the short space of life allowed him. Loving, innocent, sensitive, secluded from the vulgar concerns of his companions, strongly moralized after a peculiar and inborn type of excellence, drawing his inspirations from Nature and from his own soul in solitude, Shelley passed across the stage of this world, attended by a splendid vision which sustained him at a perilous height above the kindly race of men. The penalty of this isolation he suffered in many painful episodes. The reward he reaped in a measure of more authentic prophecy, and in a nobler realization of his best self, than could be claimed by any of his immediate contemporaries.

CHAPTER 2

ETON AND OXFORD

IN 1805 Shelley went from Sion House to Eton. At this time Dr. Keate was headmaster and Shelley's tutor was a Mr. Bethel, "one of the dullest men in the establishment." At Eton Shelley was not popular either with his teachers or his elder school-fellows, although the boys of his own age are said to have adored him. "He was all passion," writes Mrs. Shelley; "passionate in his resistance to an injury, passionate in his love:" and this vehemence of temperament he displayed by organizing a rebellion against fagging, which no doubt won for him the applause of his juniors and equals. It was not to be expected that a lad intolerant of rule and disregardful of restriction, who neglected punctuality in the performance of his exercises, while he spent his leisure in translating half of Pliny's history, should win the approbation of pedagogues. At the same time the inspired opponent of the fagging system, the scorner of games and muscular amusements, could not hope to find much favour with such martinets of juvenile convention as a public school is wont to breed. At Eton, as elsewhere, Shelley's uncompromising spirit brought him into inconvenient contact with a world of vulgar usage, while his lively fancy invested the commonplaces of reality with dark hues borrowed from his own imagination. Mrs. Shelley says of him, "Tamed by affection, but unconquered by blows, what chance was there that Shelley should be happy at a public school?" This sentence probably contains the pith of what he afterwards remembered of his own school life, and there is no doubt that a nature like his, at once loving and high-spirited, had much to suffer. It was a mistake, however, to suppose that at Eton there were any serious blows to bear, or to assume that laws of love which might have led a spirit so gentle as Shelley's, were adapted to the common stuff of which the English boy is formed. The latter mistake Shelley made continually throughout his youth; and only the advance of years tempered his passionate enthusiasm into a sober zeal for the improvement of mankind by rational methods. We may also trace at this early epoch of his life that untamed intellectual ambition—that neglect of the immediate and detailed for the transcendental and universal—which was a marked characteristic of his genius, leading him to fly at the highest while he overleaped the facts of ordinary human life. "From his earliest years," says Mrs. Shelley, "all his amusements and occupations were of a daring, and in one sense of the term, lawless nature. He delighted to exert his powers, not as a boy, but as a man; and so with manly powers and childish wit, he dared and achieved attempts that none of his comrades could even have conceived. His understanding and the early development of imagination never permitted him to mingle in childish plays; and his natural aversion to tyranny prevented him from paying due attention to his school duties. But he was always actively employed; and although his endeavours were prosecuted with puerile precipitancy, yet his aim and thoughts were constantly directed to those great objects which have employed the thoughts of the greatest among men; and though his studies were not followed up according to school discipline, they were not the less diligently applied to." This high-soaring ambition was the source both of his weakness and his strength in art, as well as in his commerce with the world of men. The boy who despised discipline and sought to extort her secrets from nature by magic, was destined to become the philanthropist who dreamed of revolutionizing society by eloquence, and the poet who invented in "Prometheus Unbound" forms of grandeur too colossal to be animated with dramatic life.

A strong interest in experimental science had been already excited in him at Sion House by the exhibition of an orrery; and this interest grew into a passion at Eton. Experiments in chemistry and electricity, of the simpler and more striking kind, gave him intense pleasure—the more so perhaps because they were forbidden. On one occasion he set the trunk of an old tree on fire with a burning-glass: on another, while he was amusing himself with a blue flame, his tutor came into the room and received a severe shock from a highly-charged Leyden jar. During the holidays Shelley carried on the same pursuits at Field Place. "His own hands and clothes," says Miss Shelley, "were constantly stained and corroded with acids, and it only seemed too probable that some day the house would be burned down, or some serious mischief happen to himself or others from the explosion of combustibles." This taste for science Shelley long retained. If we may trust Mr. Hogg's memory, the first conversation which that friend had with him at Oxford consisted almost wholly of an impassioned monologue from Shelley on the revolution to be wrought by science in all realms of thought. His imagination was fascinated by the boundless vistas opened to the student of chemistry. When he first discovered that the four elements were not final, it gave him the acutest pleasure: and this is highly characteristic of the genius which was always seeking to transcend and reach the life of life withdrawn from ordinary gaze. On the other hand he seems to have delighted in the toys of science, playing with a solar microscope, and mixing strangest compounds in his crucibles, without taking the trouble to study any of its branches systematically. In his later years he abandoned these pursuits. But a charming reminiscence of them occurs in that most delightful of his familiar poems, the "Letter to Maria Gisborne."

While translating Pliny and dabbling in chemistry, Shelley was not wholly neglectful of Etonian studies. He acquired a fluent, if not a correct, knowledge of both Greek and Latin, and astonished his contemporaries by the facility with which he produced verses in the latter language. His powers of memory were extraordinary, and the rapidity with which he read a book, taking in seven or eight lines at a glance, and seizing the sense upon the hint of leading words, was no less astonishing. Impatient speed and indifference to minutiae were indeed among the cardinal qualities of his intellect. To them we may trace not only the swiftness of his imaginative flight, but also his frequent satisfaction with the somewhat less than perfect in artistic execution.

That Shelley was not wholly friendless or unhappy at Eton may be gathered from numerous small circumstances. Hogg says that his Oxford rooms were full of handsome leaving books, and that he was frequently visited by old Etonian acquaintances. We are also told that he spend the 40 pounds gained by his first novel, "Zastrozzi," on a farewell supper to eight school-boy friends. A few lines, too, might be quoted from his own poem, the "Boat on the Serchio," to prove that he did not entertain a merely disagreeable memory of his school life. (Forman's edition, volume 4 page 115.) Yet the general experience of Eton must have been painful; and it is sad to read of this gentle and pure spirit being goaded by his coarser comrades into fury, or coaxed to curse his father and the king for their amusement. It may be worth mentioning that he was called "the Atheist" at Eton; and though Hogg explains this by saying that "the Atheist" was an official character among the boys, selected from time to time for his defiance of authority, yet it is not improbable that Shelley's avowed opinions may even then have won for him a title which he proudly claimed in after-life. To allude to his boyish incantations and nocturnal commerce with fiends and phantoms would scarcely be needful, were it not that they seem to have deeply tinged his imagination. While describing the growth of his own genius in the "Hymn to Intellectual Beauty," he makes the following reference to circumstances which might otherwise be trivial:—

> While yet a boy, I sought for ghosts, and sped
> Thro' many a listening chamber, cave, and ruin,
> And starlight wood, with fearful steps pursuing
> Hopes of high talk with the departed dead.
> I call'd on poisonous names with which our youth is fed,
> I was not heard, I saw them not—
> When, musing deeply on the lot
> Of life, at that sweet time when winds are wooing
> All vital things that wake to bring
> News of birds and blossoming,—
> Sudden, thy shadow fell on me;
> I shrieked, and clasped my hands in ecstasy!

Among the Eton tutors was one whose name will always be revered by Shelley's worshippers; for he alone discerned the rare gifts of the strange and solitary boy, and Shelley loved him. Dr. Lind was an old man, a physician, and a student of chemistry. Shelley spent long hours at his house, conversing with him, and receiving such instruction in philosophy and science as the grey-haired scholar could impart. The affection which united them must have been of no common strength or quality; for when Shelley lay ill of a fever at Field Place, and had conceived the probably ill-founded notion that his father intended to place him in a mad-house, he managed to convey a message to his friend at Eton, on the receipt of which Dr. Lind travelled to Horsham, and by his sympathy and skill restored the sick boy's confidence. It may incidentally be pointed out that this story, credited as true by Lady Shelley in her Memorials, shows how early an estrangement had begun between the poet and his father. We look, moreover, vainly for that mother's influence which might have been so beneficial to the boy in whom "love and life were twins, born at one birth." From Dr. Lind Shelley not only received encouragement to pursue his chemical studies; but he also acquired the habit of corresponding with persons unknown to him, whose opinions he might be anxious to discover or dispute. This habit, as we shall see in the sequel, determined Shelley's fate on two important occasions of his life. In return for the help extended to him at Eton, Shelley conferred undying fame on Dr. Lind; the characters of Zonaras in "Prince Athanase," and of the hermit in "Laon and Cythna," are portraits painted by the poet of his boyhood's friend.

The months which elapsed between Eton and Oxford were an important period in Shelley's life. At this time a boyish liking for his cousin, Harriet Grove, ripened into real attachment; and though there was perhaps no formal engagement between them, the parents on both sides looked with approval on their love. What it concerns us to know about this early passion, is given in a letter from a brother of Miss Grove. "Bysshe was at that time (just after leaving Eton) more attached to my sister Harriet than I can express, and I recollect well the moonlight walks we four had at Strode and also at St. Irving's; that, I think, was the name of the place, then the Duke of Norfolk's, at Horsham." For some time after the date mentioned in this letter, Shelley and Miss Grove kept up an active correspondence; but the views he expressed on speculative subjects soon began to alarm her. She consulted her mother and her father, and the engagement was broken off. The final separation does not seem to have taken place until the date of Shelley's expulsion from Oxford; and not the least cruel of the pangs he had to suffer at that period, was the loss of one to whom he had given his whole heart unreservedly. The memory of Miss Grove long continued to haunt his imagination, nor is there much doubt that his first unhappy marriage was contracted while the wound remained unhealed. The name of Harriet Westbrook and something in her face reminded him of Harriet Grove; it is even still uncertain to which Harriet the dedication of Queen Mab is addressed. (See Medwin, volume 1 page 68.)

In his childhood Shelley scribbled verses with fluency by no means unusual in the case of forward boys; and we have seen that at Sion House he greedily devoured the sentimental novels of the day. His favourite poets at the time of which I am now writing, were Monk Lewis and Southey; his favourite books in prose were romances by Mrs. Radcliffe and Godwin. He now began to yearn for fame and publicity. Miss Shelley speaks of a play written by her brother and her sister Elizabeth, which was sent to Matthews the comedian, and courteously returned as unfit for acting. She also mentions a little volume of her own verses, which the boy had printed with the tell-tale name of "H-ll-n Sh-ll-y" on the title-page. Medwin gives a long account of a poem on the story of the Wandering Jew, composed by him in concert with Shelley during the winter of 1809-1810. They sent the manuscript to Thomas Campbell, who returned it with the observation that it contained but two good lines:—

It seemed as if an angel's sigh
Had breathed the plaintive symphony.

Undeterred by this adverse criticism, Shelley subsequently offered "The Wandering Jew" to two publishers, Messrs. Ballantyne and Co. of Edinburgh, and Mr. Stockdale of Pall Mall; but it remained in MS. at Edinburgh till 1831, when a portion was printed in "Fraser's Magazine."

Just before leaving Eton he finished a novel of "Zastrozzi", which some critics trace to its source in "Zofloya the Moor," perused by him at Sion House. The most astonishing fact about this incoherent medley of mad sentiment is that it served to furnish forth the 40-pound Eton supper already spoken of, that it was duly ushered into the world of letters by Messrs. Wilkie and Robinson on the 5th of June, 1810, and that it was seriously reviewed. The dates of Shelley's publications now come fast and frequent. In the late summer of 1810 he introduced himself to Mr. J.J. Stockdale, the then fashionable publisher of poems and romances, at his house of business in Pall Mall. With characteristic impetuosity the young author implored assistance in a difficulty. He had commissioned a printer in Horsham to strike off the astounding number of 1480 copies of a volume of poems; and he had no money to pay the printer's bill. Would Stockdale help him out of this dilemma, by taking up the quires and duly ushering the book into the world? Throughout his life Shelley exercised a wonderful fascination over the people with whom he came in contact, and almost always won his way with them as much by personal charm as by determined and impassioned will. Accordingly on this occasion Stockdale proved accommodating. The Horsham printer was somehow satisfied; and on the 17th of September, 1810, the little book came out with the title of "Original Poetry, by Victor and Cazire." This volume has disappeared; and much fruitless conjecture has been expended upon the question of Shelley's collaborator in his juvenile attempt. Cazire stands for some one; probably it is meant to represent a woman's name, and that woman may have been either Elizabeth Shelley or Harriet Grove. The "Original Poetry" had only been launched a week, when Stockdale discovered on a closer inspection of the book that it contained some verses well known to the world as the production of M.G. Lewis. He immediately communicated with Shelley, and the whole edition was suppressed—not, however, before about one hundred copies had passed into circulation. To which of the collaborators this daring act of petty larceny was due, we know not; but we may be sure that Shelley satisfied Stockdale on the point of piracy, since the publisher saw no reason to break with him. On the 14th of November in the same year he issued Shelley's second novel from his press, and entered into negotiations with him for the publication of more poetry. The new romance was named "St. Irvyne, or the Rosicrucian." This tale, no less unreadable than "Zastrozzi," and even more chaotic in its plan, contained a good deal of poetry, which has been incorporated in the most recent editions of Shelley's works. A certain interest attaches to it as the first known link between Shelley and William Godwin, for it was composed under the influence of the latter's novel, "St. Leon." The title, moreover, carries us back to those moonlight walks with Harriet Grove alluded to above. Shelley's earliest attempts in literature have but little value for the student of poetry, except in so far as they illustrate the psychology of genius and its wayward growth. Their intrinsic merit is almost less than nothing, and no one could predict from their perusal the course which the future poet of "The Cenci" and "Epipsychidion" was to take.

It might indeed be argued that the defects of his great qualities, the over-ideality, the haste, the incoherence, and the want of grasp on narrative, are glaringly apparent in these early works. But while this is true, the qualities themselves are absent. A cautious critic will only find food in "Zastrozzi" and "St. Irvyne" for wondering how such flowers and fruits of genius could have lain concealed within a germ apparently so barren. There is even less of the real Shelley discernible in these productions, than of the real Byron in the "Hours of Idleness."

In the Michaelmas Term of 1810 Shelley was matriculated as a Commoner of University College, Oxford; and very soon after his arrival he made the acquaintance of a man who was destined to play a prominent part in his subsequent history, and to bequeath to posterity the most brilliant, if not in all respects the most trustworthy, record of his marvellous youth. Thomas Jefferson Hogg was unlike Shelley in temperament and tastes. His feet were always planted on the earth, while Shelley flew aloft to heaven with singing robes around him, or the mantel of the prophet on his shoulders. (He told Trelawny that he had been attracted to Shelley simply by his "rare talents as a scholar;" and Trelawny has recorded his opinion that Hogg's portrait of their friend was faithful, in spite of a total want of sympathy with his poetic genius. This testimony is extremely valuable.) Hogg had much of the cynic in his nature; he was a shrewd man of the world, and a caustic humorist. Positive and practical, he chose the beaten path of life, rose to eminence as a lawyer, and cherished the Church and State opinions of a staunch Tory. Yet, though he differed so essentially from the divine poet, he understood the greatness of Shelley at a glance, and preserved for us a record of his friend's early days, which is incomparable for the vividness of its portraiture. The pages which narrate Shelley's course of life at Oxford have all the charm of a romance. No novel indeed is half so delightful as that picture, at once affectionate and satirical, tender and humorous, extravagant and delicately shaded, of the student life enjoyed together for a few short months by the inseparable friends. To make extracts from a masterpiece of such consummate workmanship is almost painful. Future biographers of Shelley, writing on a scale adequate to the greatness of their subject, will be content to lay their pens down for a season at this point, and let Hogg tell the tale in his own wayward but inimitable fashion. I must confine myself to a few quotations and a barren abstract, referring my readers to the ever-memorable pages 48—286 of Hogg's first volume, for the life that cannot be transferred to these.

"At the commencement of Michaelmas term," says this biographer, "that is, at the end of October, in the year 1810, I happened one day to sit next to a freshman at dinner; it was his first appearance in hall. His figure was slight, and his aspect remarkably youthful, even at our table, where all were very young. He seemed thoughtful and absent. He ate little, and had no acquaintance with any one." The two young men began a conversation, which turned upon the respective merits of German and Italian poetry, a subject they neither of them knew anything about. After dinner it was continued in Hogg's rooms, where

Shelley soon led the talk to his favourite topic of science. "As I felt, in truth, but a slight interest in the subject of his conversation, I had leisure to examine, and I may add, to admire, the appearance of my very extraordinary guest. It was a sum of many contradictions. His figure was slight and fragile, and yet his bones and joints were large and strong. He was tall, but he stooped so much, that he seemed of a low stature. His clothes were expensive, and made according to the most approved mode of the day; but they were tumbled, rumpled, unbrushed. His gestures were abrupt, and sometimes violent, occasionally even awkward, yet more frequently gentle and graceful. His complexion was delicate and almost feminine, of the purest red and white; yet he was tanned and freckled by exposure to the sun, having passed the autumn, as he said, in shooting. His features, his whole face, and particularly his head, were, in fact, unusually small; yet the last APPEARED of a remarkable bulk, for his hair was long and bushy, and in fits of absence, and in the agonies (if I may use the word) of anxious thought, he often rubbed it fiercely with his hands, or passed his fingers quickly through his locks unconsciously, so that it was singularly wild and rough. In times when it was the mode to imitate stage-coachmen as closely as possible in costume, and when the hair was invariably cropped, like that of our soldiers, this eccentricity was very striking. His features were not symmetrical (the mouth, perhaps, excepted), yet was the effect of the whole extremely powerful. They breathed an animation, a fire, an enthusiasm, a vivid and preternatural intelligence, that I never met with in any other countenance. Nor was the moral expression less beautiful than the intellectual; for there was a softness, a delicacy, a gentleness, and especially (though this will surprise many) that air of profound religious veneration, that characterizes the best works, and chiefly the frescoes (and into these they infused their whole souls), of the great masters of Florence and of Rome. I recognized the very peculiar expression in these wonderful productions long afterwards, and with a satisfaction mingled with much sorrow, for it was after the decease of him in whose countenance I had first observed it."

In another place Hogg gives some details which complete the impression of Shelley's personal appearance, and which are fully corroborated by Trelawny's recollections of a later date. "There were many striking contrasts in the character and behaviour of Shelley, and one of the most remarkable was a mixture, or alternation, of awkwardness with agility—of the clumsy with the graceful. He would stumble in stepping across the floor of a drawing room; he would trip himself up on a smooth-shaven grass-plot, and he would tumble in the most inconceivable manner in ascending the commodious, facile, and well-carpeted staircase of an elegant mansion, so as to bruise his nose or his lip on the upper steps, or to tread upon his hands, and even occasionally to disturb the composure of a well-bred footman; on the contrary, he would often glide without collision through a crowded assembly, thread with unerring dexterity a most intricate path, or securely and rapidly tread the most arduous and uncertain ways."

This word-portrait corresponds in its main details to the descriptions furnished by other biographers, who had the privilege of Shelley's friendship.

His eyes were blue, unfathomably dark and lustrous. His hair was brown; but very early in life it became grey, while his unwrinkled face retained to the last a look of wonderful youth. It is admitted on all sides that no adequate picture was ever painted of him. Mulready is reported to have said that he was too beautiful to paint. And yet, although so singularly lovely, he owed less of his charm to regularity of feature or to grace of movement, than to an indescribable personal fascination. One further detail Hogg pointedly insists upon. Shelley's voice "was excruciating; it was intolerably shrill, harsh and discordant." This is strongly stated; but, though the terms are certainly exaggerated, I believe that we must trust this first impression made on Shelley's friend. There is a considerable mass of convergent testimony to the fact that Shelley's voice was high pitched, and that when he became excited, he raised it to a scream. The epithets "shrill," "piercing," "penetrating," frequently recur in the descriptions given of it. At the same time its quality seems to have been less dissonant than thrilling; there is abundance of evidence to prove that he could modulate it exquisitely in the reading of poetry, and its tone proved no obstacle to the persuasive charms of his eloquence in conversation. Like all finely tempered natures, he vibrated in harmony with the subjects of his thought. Excitement made his utterance shrill and sharp. Deep feeling of the sense of beauty lowered its tone to richness; but the timbre was always acute, in sympathy with his intense temperament. All was of one piece in Shelley's nature. This peculiar voice, varying from moment to moment, and affecting different sensibilities in divers ways, corresponds to the high-strung passion of his life, his fine-drawn and ethereal fancies, and the clear vibrations of his palpitating verse. Such a voice, far-reaching, penetrating, and unearthly, befitted one who lived in rarest ether on the topmost heights of human thought.

The acquaintance begun that October evening soon ripened into close friendship. Shelley and Hogg from this time forward spent a large part of their days and nights together in common studies, walks and conversations. It was their habit to pass the morning, each in his own rooms, absorbed in private reading. At one o'clock they met and lunched, and then started for long rambles in the country. Shelley frequently carried pistols with him upon these occasions, and would stop to fix his father's franks upon convenient trees and shoot at them. The practice of pistol shooting, adopted so early in life, was afterwards one of his favourite amusements in the company of Byron. Hogg says that in his use of fire-arms he was extraordinarily careless. "How often have I lamented that Nature, which so rarely bestows upon the world a creature endowed with such marvellous talents, ungraciously rendered the gift less precious by implanting a fatal taste for perilous recreations, and a thoughtlessness in the pursuit of them, that often caused his existence from one day to another to seem in itself miraculous." On their return from these excursions the two friends, neither of whom cared for dining in the College Hall, drank tea and supped together, Shelley's rooms being generally chosen as the scene of their symposia.

These rooms are described as a perfect palace of confusion—chaos on chaos heaped of chemical apparatus, books, electrical machines, unfinished manuscripts, and furniture worn into holes by acids. It was perilous to use the poet's drinking-vessels, less perchance a seven-shilling piece half dissolved in aqua regia should lurk at the bottom of the bowl. Handsome razors were used to cut the lids of wooden boxes, and valuable books served to support lamps or crucibles; for in his vehement precipitation Shelley always laid violent hands on what he found convenient to the purpose of the moment. Here the friends talked and read until late in the night. Their chief studies at this time were in Locke and Hume and the French essayists. Shelley's bias toward metaphysical speculation was beginning to assert itself. He read the School Logic with avidity, and practised himself without intermission in dialectical discussion. Hogg observes, what is confirmed by other testimony, that in reasoning Shelley never lost sight of the essential bearings of the topic in dispute, never condescended to personal or captious arguments, and was Socratically bent on following the dialogue wherever it might lead, without regard for consequences. Plato was another of their favourite authors; but Hogg expressly tells us that they only approached the divine philosopher through the medium of translations. It was not until a later period that Shelley studied his dialogues in the original: but the substance of them, seen through Mdme. Dacier's version, acted powerfully on the poet's sympathetic intellect. In fact, although at the time he had adopted the conclusions of materialism, he was at heart all through his life an idealist. Therefore the mixture of the poet and the sage in Plato fascinated him. The doctrine of anamnesis, which offers so strange a vista to speculative reverie, by its suggestion of an earlier existence in which our knowledge was acquired, took a strong hold upon his imagination; he would stop in the streets to gaze wistfully at babies, wondering whether their newly imprisoned souls were not replete with the wisdom stored up in a previous life.

In the acquisition of knowledge he was then as ever unrelaxing. "No student ever read more assiduously. He was to be found, book in hand, at all hours; reading in season and out of season; at table, in bed, and especially during a walk; not only in the quiet country, and in retired paths; not only at Oxford, in the public walks, and High Street, but in the most crowded thoroughfares of London. Nor was he less absorbed by the volume that was open before him, in Cheapside, in Cranbourne Alley, or in Bond Street, than in a lonely lane, or a secluded library. Sometimes a vulgar fellow would attempt to insult or annoy the eccentric student in passing. Shelley always avoided the malignant interruption by stepping aside with his vast and quiet agility." And again:—"I never beheld eyes that devoured the pages more voraciously than his; I am convinced that two-thirds of the period of the day and night were often employed in reading. It is no exaggeration to affirm, that out of twenty-four hours, he frequently read sixteen. At Oxford, his diligence in this respect was exemplary, but it greatly increased afterwards, and I sometimes thought that he carried it to a pernicious excess: I am sure, at least, that I was unable to keep pace with him." With Shelley study was a passion, and the acquisition of knowledge was the entrance into a thrice-hallowed sanctuary. "The irreverent many cannot comprehend the awe—the careless apathetic worldling cannot imagine the enthusiasm—nor can the tongue that attempts only to speak of things visible to the bodily eye, express the mighty emotion that inwardly agitated him, when he approached, for the first time, a volume which he believed to be replete with the recondite and mystic philosophy of antiquity: his cheeks glowed, his eyes became bright, his whole frame trembled, and his entire attention was immediately swallowed up in the depths of contemplation. The rapid and vigorous conversion of his soul to intellect can only be compared with the instantaneous ignition and combustion, which dazzle the sight, when a bundle of dry reeds, or other light inflammable substance, is thrown upon a fire already rich with accumulated heat."

As at Eton, so at Oxford, Shelley refused to keep the beaten track of prescribed studies, or to run in ordinary grooves of thought. The mere fact that Aristotle was a duty, seems to have disgusted him with the author of the Organon, from whom, had his works been prohibited to undergraduates, he would probably have been eager to learn much. For mathematics and jurisprudence he evinced a marked distaste. The common business of the English Parliament had no attraction for him, and he read few newspapers. While his mind was keenly interested in great political questions, he could not endure the trivial treatment of them in the daily press, and cared far more for principles than for the incidents of party warfare. Here again he showed that impatience of detail, and that audacity of self-reliant genius, which were the source of both his weakness and his strength. He used to speak with aversion of a Parliamentary career, and told Hogg that though this had been suggested to him, as befitting his position, by the Duke of Norfolk, he could never bring himself to mix with the rabble of the House. It is none the less true, however, that he entertained some vague notion of eventually succeeding to his father's seat.

Combined with his eager intellectual activity, there was something intermittent and fitful in the working of his mental faculties. Hogg, in particular, mentions one of his habits in a famous passage, which, since it brings the two friends vividly before us, may here be quoted. "I was enable to continue my studies afterwards in the evening, in consequence of a very remarkable peculiarity. My young and energetic friend was then overcome by extreme drowsiness, which speedily and completely vanquished him; he would sleep from two to four hours, often so soundly that his slumbers resembled a deep lethargy; he lay occasionally upon the sofa, but more commonly stretched upon the rug before a large fire, like a cat; and his little round head was exposed to such a fierce heat, that I used to wonder how he was able to bear it. Sometimes I have interposed some shelter, but rarely with any permanent effect; for the sleeper usually contrived to turn himself, and to roll again into the spot where the fire glowed the brightest. His torpor was generally profound, but he would sometimes discourse incoherently for a long while in his sleep. At six he would suddenly compose himself, even in the midst of a most animated narrative, or of earnest discussion; and he would lie buried in entire forgetfulness, in a sweet and mighty oblivion, until ten, when he would suddenly start up, and, rubbing his eyes with great violence, and passing his fingers swiftly through his long hair, would enter at once into a vehement argument, or begin to recite verses, either of his own composition or from the works of others, with a rapidity and an energy that were often quite painful."

Shelley's moral qualities are described with no less enthusiasm than his intellectual and physical beauty by the friend from whom I have already drawn so largely. Love was the root and basis of his nature: this love, first developed as domestic affection, next as friendship, then as a youth's passion, now began to shine with steady lustre as an all-embracing devotion to his fellow-men. There is something inevitably chilling in the words "benevolence" and "philanthropy." A disillusioned world is inclined to look with languid approbation on the former, and to disbelieve in the latter. Therefore I will not use them to describe that intense and glowing passion of unselfishness, which throughout his life led Shelley to find his strongest interests in the joys and sorrows of his fellow-creatures, which inflamed his imagination with visions of humanity made perfect, and which filled his days with sweet deeds of unnumbered charities. I will rather collect from the page of his friend's biography a few passages recording the first impression of his character, the memory of which may be carried by the reader through the following brief record of his singular career:—

"His speculations were as wild as the experience of twenty-one years has shown them to be; but the zealous earnestness for the augmentation of knowledge, and the glowing philanthropy and boundless benevolence that marked them, and beamed forth in the whole deportment of that extraordinary boy, are not less astonishing than they would have been if the whole of his glorious anticipations had been prophetic; for these high qualities, at least, I have never found a parallel."

"In no individual perhaps was the moral sense ever more completely developed than in Shelley; in no being was the perception of right and of wrong more acute."

"As his love of intellectual pursuits was vehement, and the vigour of his genius almost celestial, so were the purity and sanctity of his life most conspicuous."

"I never knew any one so prone to admire as he was, in whom the principle of veneration was so strong."

"I have had the happiness to associate with some of the best specimens of gentlemen; but with all due deference for those admirable persons (may my candour and my preference be pardoned), I can affirm that Shelley was almost the only example I have yet found that was never wanting, even in the most minute particular, of the infinite and various observances of pure, entire, and perfect gentility."

"Shelley was actually offended, and indeed more indignant than would appear to be consistent with the singular mildness of his nature, at a coarse and awkward jest, especially if it were immodest, or uncleanly; in the latter case his anger was unbounded, and his uneasiness pre-eminent; he was, however, sometimes vehemently delighted by exquisite and delicate sallies, particularly with a fanciful, and perhaps somewhat fantastical facetiousness—possibly the more because he was himself utterly incapable of pleasantry."

"I could never discern in him any more than two fixed principles. The first was a strong irrepressible love of liberty; of liberty in the abstract, and somewhat after the pattern of the ancient republics, without reference to the English constitution, respecting which he knew little and cared nothing, heeding it not at all. The second was an equally ardent love of toleration of all opinions, but more especially of religious opinions; of toleration, complete, entire, universal, unlimited; and, as a deduction and corollary from which latter principle, he felt an intense abhorrence of persecution of every kind, public or private."

The testimony in the foregoing extracts as to Shelley's purity and elevation of moral character is all the stronger, because it is given by a man not over-inclined to praise, and of a temperament as unlike the poet's as possible. If we were to look only upon this side of his portrait, we should indeed be almost forced to use the language of his most enthusiastic worshippers, and call him an archangel. But it must be admitted that, though so pure and gentle and exalted, Shelley's virtues were marred by his eccentricity, by something at times approaching madness, which paralyzed his efficiency by placing him in a glaringly false relation to some of the best men in the world around him. He possessed certain good qualities in excess; for, though it sounds paradoxical, it is none the less true that a man may be too tolerant, too fond of liberty: and it was precisely the extravagance of these virtues in Shelley which drove him into acts and utterances so antagonistic to society as to be intolerable.

Of Shelley's poetical studies we hear but little at this epoch. His genius by a stretch of fancy might be compared to one of those double stars which dart blue and red rays of light: for it was governed by two luminaries, poetry and metaphysics; and at this time the latter seems to have been in the ascendant. It is, however, interesting to learn that he read and re-read Landor's "Gebir"— stronger meat than either Southey's epics or the ghost-lyrics of Monk Lewis. Hogg found him one day busily engaged in correcting proofs of some original poems. Shelley asked his friend what he thought of them, and Hogg answered that it might be possible by a little alteration to turn them into capital burlesques. The idea took the young poet's fancy; and the friends between them soon effected a metamorphosis in Shelley's serious verses, by which they became unmistakably ridiculous. Having achieved their purpose, they now bethought them of the proper means of publication. Upon whom should the poems, a medley of tyrannicide and revolutionary raving, be fathered? Peg Nicholson, a mad washerwoman, had recently attempted George the Third's life with a carving-knife. No more fitting author could be found. They would give their pamphlet to the world as her work, edited by an admiring nephew. The printer appreciated the joke no less than the authors of it. He provided splendid paper and magnificent type; and before long the book of nonsense was in the hands of Oxford readers. It sold for the high price of half-a-crown a copy; and, what is hardly credible, the gownsmen received it as a genuine production. "It was indeed a kind of fashion to be seen reading it in public, as a mark of nice discernment, of a delicate and fastidious taste in poetry, and the best criterion of a choice spirit." Such was the genesis of "Posthumous Fragments of Margaret Nicholson", edited by John Fitz Victor. The name of the supposititious nephew reminds us of "Original Poems" by Victor and Cazire, and raises the question whether the poems in that lost volume may not have partly furnished forth this Oxford travesty.

Shelley's next publication, or quasi-publication, was neither so innocent in substance nor so pleasant in its consequences. After leaving Eton, he continued the habit, learned from Dr. Lind, of corresponding with distinguished persons whom he did not personally know. Thus we find him about this time addressing Miss Felicia Browne (afterwards Mrs. Hemans) and Leigh Hunt. He plied his correspondents with all kinds of questions; and as the dialectical interest was uppermost at Oxford, he now endeavoured to engage them in discussions on philosophical and religious topics. We have seen that his favourite authors were Locke, Hume, and the French materialists. With the impulsiveness peculiar to his nature, he adopted the negative conclusions of a shallow nominalistic philosophy. It was a fundamental point with him to regard all questions, however sifted and settled by the wise of former ages, as still open; and in his inordinate thirst for liberty, he rejoiced to be the Deicide of a pernicious theological delusion. In other words, he passed at Oxford by one leap from a state of indifferentism with regard to Christianity, into an attitude of vehement antagonism. With a view to securing answers to his missives, he printed a short abstract of Hume's and other arguments against the existence of a Deity, presented in a series of propositions, and signed with a mathematically important "Q.E.D." This document he forwarded to his proposed antagonists, expressing his inability to answer its arguments, and politely requesting them to help him. When it so happened that any incautious correspondents acceded to this appeal, Shelley fell with merciless severity upon their feeble and commonplace reasoning. The little pamphlet of two pages was entitled "The Necessity of Atheism"; and its proposed publication, beyond the limits of private circulation already described, is proved by an advertisement (February 9, 1811) in the "Oxford University and City Herald". It was not, however, actually offered for sale.

A copy of this syllabus reached a Fellow of another college, who made the Master of the University acquainted with the fact. On the morning of March 25, 1811, Shelley was sent for to the Senior Common Room, and asked whether he acknowledged himself to be the author of the obnoxious pamphlet. On his refusal to answer this question, he was served with a formal sentence of expulsion duly drawn up and sealed. The college authorities have been blamed for unfair dealing in this matter. It is urged that they ought to have proceeded by the legal method of calling witnesses; and that the sentence was not only out of all proportion to the offence, but that it ought not to have been executed till persuasion had been tried. With regard to the former indictment, I do not think that a young man still in statu pupillari, who refused to purge himself of what he must have known to be a serious charge, had any reason to expect from his tutors the formalities of an English court of law. There is no doubt that the

Fellows were satisfied of his being the real author; else they could not have ventured on so summary a measure as expulsion. Their question was probably intended to give the culprit an occasion for apology, of which they foresaw he would not avail himself. With regard to the second, it is true that Shelley was amenable to kindness, and that gentle and wise treatment from men whom he respected might possibly have brought him to retract his syllabus. But it must be remembered that he despised the Oxford dons with all his heart; and they were probably aware of this. He was a dexterous, impassioned reasoner, whom they little cared to encounter in argument on such a topic. During his short period of residence, moreover, he had not shown himself so tractable as to secure the good wishes of superiors, who prefer conformity to incommensurable genius. It is likely that they were not averse to getting rid of him as a man dangerous to the peace of their society; and now they had a good occasion. Nor was it to be expected that the champion and apostle of Atheism—and Shelley was certainly both, in spite of Hogg's attempts to tone down the purpose of his document— should be unmolested in his propaganda by the aspirants to fat livings and ecclesiastical dignities. Real blame, however, attaches to these men: first, for their dulness to discern Shelley's amiable qualities; and, secondly, for the prejudgment of the case implied in the immediate delivery of their sentence. Both Hogg and Shelley accused them, besides, of a gross brutality, which was, to say the least, unseemly on so serious an occasion. At the beginning of this century the learning and the manners of Oxford dons were at a low ebb; and the Fellows of University College acted harshly but not altogether unjustly, ignorantly but after their own kind, in this matter of Shelley's expulsion. $Non ragionem di lor, ma guarda e passa. Hogg, who stood by his friend manfully at this crisis, and dared the authorities to deal with him as they had dealt with Shelley, adding that they had just as much real proof to act upon in his case, and intimating his intention of returning the same answer as to the authorship of the pamphlet, was likewise expelled. The two friends left Oxford together by coach on the morning of the 26th of March.

Shelley felt his expulsion acutely. At Oxford he had enjoyed the opportunities of private reading which the University afforded in those days of sleepy studies and innocuous examinations. He delighted in the security of his "oak," and above all things he found pleasure in the society of his one chosen friend. He was now obliged to exchange these good things for the tumult and discomfort of London. His father, after clumsily attempting compromises, had forbidden his return to Field Place. The whole fabric of his former life was broken up. The last hope of renewing his engagement with his cousin had to be abandoned. His pecuniary position was precarious, and in a short time he was destined to lose the one friend who had so generously shared his fate. Yet the notion of recovering his position as a student in one of our great Universities, of softening his father's indignation, or of ameliorating his present circumstances by the least concession, never seems to have occurred to him. He had suffered in the cause of truth and liberty, and he willingly accepted his martyrdom for conscience' sake.

CHAPTER 3

LIFE IN LONDON AND FIRST MARRIAGE

IT is of some importance at this point to trace the growth and analyse the substance of Shelley's atheistical opinions. The cardinal characteristic of his nature was an implacable antagonism to shams and conventions, which passed too easily into impatient rejection of established forms as worse than useless. Born in the stronghold of squirearchical prejudices, nursed amid the trivial platitudes that then passed in England for philosophy, his keen spirit flew to the opposite pole of thought with a recoil that carried him at first to inconsiderate negation. His passionate love of liberty, his loathing for intolerance, his impatience of control for self and others, and his vivid logical sincerity, combined to make him the Quixotic champion of extreme opinions. He was too fearless to be wise, too precipitate to suspend his judgment, too convinced of the paramount importance of iconoclasm, to mature his views in silence. With the unbounded audacity of youth, he hoped to take the fortresses of "Anarch Custom" by storm at the first assault. His favourite ideal was the vision of a youth, Laon or Lionel, whose eloquence had power to break the bonds of despotism, as the sun thaws ice upon an April morning. It was enough, he thought, to hurl the glove of defiance boldly at the tyrant's face—to sow the "Necessity of Atheism" broadcast on the bench of Bishops, and to depict incest in his poetry, not because he wished to defend it, but because society must learn to face the most abhorrent problems with impartiality. Gifted with a touch as unerring as Ithuriel's spear for the unmasking of hypocrisy, he strove to lay bare the very substance of the soul beneath the crust of dogma and the froth of traditional beliefs; nor does it seem to have occurred to him that, while he stripped the rags and patches that conceal the nakedness of ordinary human nature, he might drag away the weft and woof of nobler thought. In his poet-philosopher's imagination there bloomed a wealth of truth and love and beauty so abounding, that behind the mirage he destroyed, he saw no blank, but a new Eternal City of the Spirit. He never doubted whether his fellow-creatures were certain to be equally fortunate.

Shelley had no faculty for compromise, no perception of the blended truths and falsehoods through which the mind of man must gradually win its way from the obscurity of myths into the clearness of positive knowledge, for ever toiling and for ever foiled, and forced to content itself with the increasing consciousness of limitations. Brimming over with love for men, he was deficient in sympathy with the conditions under which they actually think and feel. Could he but dethrone the Anarch Custom, the millennium, he argued, would immediately arrive; nor did he stop to think how different was the fibre of his own soul from that of the unnumbered multitudes around him. In his adoration of what he recognized as living, he retained no reverence for the ossified experience of past ages. The principle of evolution, which forms a saving link between the obsolete and the organically vital, had no place in his logic. The spirit of the French Revolution, uncompromising, shattering, eager to build in a day the structure which long centuries of growth must fashion, was still fresh upon him. We who have survived the enthusiasm of that epoch, who are exhausted with its passions, and who have suffered from its reactive impulses, can scarcely comprehend the vivid faith and young-eyed joy of aspiration which sustained Shelley in his flight toward the region of impossible ideals. For he had a vital faith; and this faith made the ideals he conceived seem possible—faith in the duty and desirability of overthrowing idols; faith in the gospel of liberty, fraternity, equality; faith in the divine beauty of nature; faith in a love that rules the universe; faith in the perfectibility of man; faith in the omnipresent soul, whereof our souls are atoms; faith in affection as the ruling and co-ordinating substance of morality. The man who lived by this faith was in no vulgar sense of the word an Atheist. When he proclaimed himself to be one, he pronounced his hatred of a gloomy religion, which had been the instrument of kings and priests for the enslavement of their fellow-creatures. As he told his friend Trelawny, he used the word Atheism "to express his abhorrence of superstition; he took it up as a knight took up a gauntlet, in defiance of injustice." But Shelley believed too much to be consistently agnostic. He believed so firmly and intensely in his own religion—a kind of passionate positivism, a creed which seemed to have no God because it was all God—that he felt convinced he only needed to destroy accepted figments, for the light which blazed around him to break through and flood the world with beauty. Shelley can only be called an Atheist, in so far as he maintained the inadequacy of hitherto received conceptions of the Deity, and indignantly rejected that Moloch of cruelty who is worshipped in the debased forms of Christianity. He was an Agnostic only in so far as he proclaimed the impossibility of solving the insoluble, and knowing the unknowable. His clear and fearless utterances upon these points place him in the rank of intellectual heroes. But his own soul, compact of human faith and love, was far too religious and too sanguine to merit either epithet as vulgarly applied.

The negative side of Shelley's creed had the moral value which attaches to all earnest conviction, plain speech, defiance of convention, and enthusiasm for intellectual liberty at any cost. It was marred, however, by extravagance, crudity, and presumption. Much that he would fain have destroyed because he found it customary, was solid, true, and beneficial. Much that he thought it desirable to substitute, was visionary, hollow, and pernicious. He lacked the touchstone of mature philosophy, whereby to separate the pinchbeck from the gold of social usage; and in his intense enthusiasm he lost his hold on common sense, which might have saved him from the puerility of arrogant iconoclasm. The positive side of his creed remains precious, not because it was logical, or scientific, or coherent, but because it was an ideal, fervently felt, and penetrated with the whole life-force of an incomparable nature. Such ideals are needed for sustaining man upon his path amid the glooms and shadows of impenetrable ignorance. The form the seal and pledge of his spiritual dignity, reminding him that he was not born to live like brutes, or like the brutes to perish without effort.

Fatti non foste a viver come bruti,
Ma per seguir virtude e conoscenza.

These criticisms apply to the speculations of Shelley's earlier life, when his crusade against accepted usage was extravagant, and his confidence in the efficacy of mere eloquence to change the world was overweening. The experience of years, however, taught him wisdom without damping his enthusiasm, refined the crudity of his first fervent speculations, and mellowed his philosophy. Had he lived to a ripe age, there is no saying with what clear and beneficent lustre might have shone that light of aspiration which during his turbid youth burned somewhat luridly, and veiled its radiance in the smoke of mere rebelliousness and contradiction.

Hogg and Shelley settled in lodgings at No. 15, Poland Street, soon after their arrival in London. The name attracted Shelley: "it reminded him of Thaddeus of Warsaw and of freedom." He was further fascinated by a gaudy wall-paper of vine-trellises and grapes, which adorned the parlour; and vowed that he would stay there for ever. "For ever," was a word often upon Shelley's lips in the course of his chequered life; and yet few men have been subject to so many sudden changes through the buffetings of fortune from without and the inconstancy of their own purpose, than he was. His biographer has no little trouble to trace and note with accuracy his perpetual flittings and the names of his innumerable temporary residences. A month had not elapsed before Hogg left him in order to begin his own law studies at York; and Shelley abode "alone in the vine-trellised chamber, where he was to remain, a bright-eyed, restless fox amidst sour grapes, not, as his poetic imagination at first suggested, for ever, but a little while longer."

The records of this first residence in London are meagre, but not unimportant. We hear of negotiations and interviews with Mr. Timothy Shelley, all of which proved unavailing. Shelley would not recede from the position he had taken up. Nothing would induce him to break off his intimacy with Hogg, or to place himself under the tutor selected for him by his father. For Paley's, or as Mr. Shelley called him "Palley's," Evidences he expressed unbounded contempt. The breach between them gradually widened. Mr. Shelley at last determined to try the effect of cutting off supplies; but his son only hardened his heart, and sustained himself by a proud consciousness of martyrdom. I agree with Shelley's last and best biographer, Mr. W.M. Rossetti, in his condemnation of the poet's behaviour as a son. Shelley did not treat his father with the common consideration due from youth to age; and the only instances of unpardonable bad taste to be found in his correspondence or the notes of his conversation, are insulting phrases applied to a man who was really more unfortunate than criminal in his relations to this changeling from the realms of faery. It is not too much to say that his dislike of his father amounted to derangement; and certainly some of his suspicions with regard to him were the hallucinations of a heated fancy. How so just and gentle a nature was brought into so false a moral situation, whether by some sudden break-down of confidence in childhood or by a gradually increasing mistrust, is an interesting but perhaps insoluble problem. We only know that in his early boyhood Shelley loved his father so much as to have shown unusual emotion during his illness on one occasion, but that, while at Eton he had already become possessed by a dark suspicion concerning him. This is proved by the episode of Dr. Lind's visit during his fever. Then and ever afterwards he expected monstrous treatment at his hands, although the elder gentleman was nothing worse than a muddle-headed squire. It has more than once occurred to me that this fever may have been a turning point in his history, and that a delusion, engendered by delirium, may have fixed itself upon his mind, owing to some imperfection in the process of recovery. But the theory is too speculative and unsupported by proof to be more than passingly alluded to.

At this time Shelley found it difficult to pay his lodgings and to buy food. It is said that his sisters saved their pocket-money to support him: and we know that he paid them frequent visits at their school on Clapham Common. It was here that his characteristic hatred of tyranny displayed itself on two occasions. "One day," writes Miss Hellen Shelley, "his ire was greatly excited at a black mark hung round one of our throats, as a penalty for some small misdemeanour. He expressed great disapprobation, more of the system than that one of his sisters should be so punished. Another time he found me, I think, in an iron collar, which certainly was a dreadful instrument of torture in my opinion. It was not worn as a punishment, but because I POKED; but Bysshe declared that it would make me grow crooked, and ought to be discontinued immediately." The acquaintance which he now made with one of his sister's school friends was destined to lead to most important results. (It is probable that he saw her for the first time in January, 1811.) Harriet Westbrook was a girl of sixteen years, remarkably good-looking, with a brilliant pink and white complexion, beautiful brown hair, a pleasant voice, and a cheerful temper. She was the daughter of a man who kept a coffee-house in Mount Street, nick-named "Jew" Westbrook, because of his appearance. She had an elder sister, called Eliza, dark of complexion, and gaunt of figure, with the abundant hair that plays so prominent a part in Hogg's relentless portrait. Eliza, being nearly twice as old as Harriet, stood in the relation of a mother to her. Both of these young ladies, and the "Jew" their father, welcomed Shelley with distinguished kindness. Though he was penniless for the nonce, exiled from his home, and under the ban of his family's displeasure, he was still the heir to a large landed fortune and a baronetcy. It was not to be expected that the coffee-house people should look upon him with disfavour.

Shelley paid Harriet frequent visits, both at Mrs. Fenning's school and at Mount Street, and soon began a correspondence with her, hoping, as he expressly stated in a letter of a later date, by converting her to his theories, to add his sister and her "to the list of the good, the disinterested and the free." At first she seems to have been horrified at the opinions he expressed; but in this case at least he did not overrate the powers of eloquence. With all the earnestness of an evangelist, he preached his gospel of freethought or atheism, and had the satisfaction of forming his young pupil to his views. He does not seem to have felt any serious inclination for Harriet; but in the absence of other friends, he gladly availed himself of her society. Gradually she became more interesting to him, when he heard mysterious accounts of suffering at home and tyranny at school. This was enough to rouse in Shelley the spirit of Quixotic championship, if not to sow the seeds of love. What Harriet's ill-treatment really was, no one has been able to discover; yet she used to affirm that her life at this time was so irksome that she contemplated suicide.

During the summer of 1811, Shelley's movements were more than usually erratic, and his mind was in a state of extraordinary restlessness. In the month of May, a kind of accommodation was come to with his father. He received permission to revisit Field Place, and had an allowance made him of 200 pounds a year. His uncle, Captain Pilfold of Cuckfield, was instrumental in effecting this partial reconciliation. Shelley spent some time at his uncle's country house, oscillating between London, Cuckfield, and Field Place, with characteristic rapidity, and paying one flying visit to his cousin Grove at Cwm Elan, near Rhayader, in North Wales. This visit is worth mention, since he now for the first time saw the scenery of waterfalls and mountains. He was, however, too much preoccupied to take much interest in nature. He was divided between his old affection for Miss Grove, his new but somewhat languid interest in Harriet, and a dearly cherished scheme for bringing about a marriage between his sister Elizabeth and his friend Hogg. The letters written to Hogg at this period (volume 1 pages 387-418) are exceedingly important and interesting, revealing as they do the perturbation of his feelings and the almost morbid excitement of his mind. But they are unluckily so badly edited, whether designedly or by accident, that it would be dangerous to draw minute conclusions from them. As they stand, they raise injurious suspicions, which can only be set at rest by a proper assignment of dates and explanation.

Meanwhile his destiny was shaping itself with a rapidity that plunged him suddenly into decisive and irrevocable action. It is of the greatest moment to ascertain precisely what his feelings were during this summer with regard to Harriet. Hogg has printed two letters in immediate juxtaposition: the first without date, the second with the post-mark of Rhayader. Shelley ends the first epistle thus: "Your jokes on Harriet Westbrook amuse me: it is a common error for people to fancy others in their own situation, but if I know anything about love, I am NOT in love. I have heard from the Westbrooks, both of whom I highly esteem." He begins the second with these words: "You will perhaps see me before you can answer this; perhaps not; heaven knows! I shall certainly come to York, but HARRIET WESTBROOK will decide whether now or in three weeks. Her father has persecuted her in a most horrible way, by endeavouring to compel her to go to school. She asked my advice: resistance was the answer, at the same time that I essayed to mollify Mr. W. in vain! And in consequence of my advice SHE has thrown herself upon MY protection. I set off for London on Monday. How flattering a distinction!—I am thinking of ten million things at once. What have I said? I declare, quite LUDICROUS. I advised her to resist. She wrote to say that resistance was useless, but that she would fly with me, and threw herself upon my protection. We shall have 200 pounds a year; when we find it run short, we must live, I suppose, upon love! Gratitude and admiration, all demand that I should love her FOR EVER. We shall see you at York. I will hear your arguments for matrimonialism, by which I am now almost convinced. I can get lodgings at York, I suppose. Direct to me at Graham's, 18 Sackville Street, Piccadilly." From a letter recently published by Mr. W.M. Rossetti (the University Magazine, February 1878), we further learn that Harriet, having fallen violently in love with her preceptor, had avowed her passion and flung herself into his arms.

It is clear from these documents, first, that Shelley was not deeply in love with Harriet when he eloped with her; secondly, that he was not prepared for the step; thirdly, that she induced him to take it; and fourthly, that he took it under a strong impression of her having been ill-treated. She had appealed to his most powerful passion, the hatred of tyranny. She had excited his admiration by setting conventions at defiance, and showing her readiness to be his mistress. Her confidence called forth his gratitude. Her choice of him for a protector flattered him: and, moreover, she had acted on his advice to carry resistance a outrance. There are many good Shelleyan reasons why he should elope with Harriet; but among them all I do not find that spontaneous and unsophisticated feeling, which is the substance of enduring love.

In the same series of letters, so incoherently jumbled together by Hogg's carelessness or caprice, Shelley more than once expresses the utmost horror of matrimony. Yet we now find him upon the verge of contracting marriage with a woman whom he did not passionately love, and who had offered herself unreservedly to him. It is worth pausing to observe that even Shelley, fearless and uncompromising as he was in conduct, could not at this crisis practise the principles he so eloquently impressed on others. Yet the point of weakness was honourable. It lay in his respect for women in general, and in his tender chivalry for the one woman who had cast herself upon his generosity. (See Shelley's third letter to Godwin (Hogg 2 page 63) for another defence of his conduct. "We agreed," etc.)

"My unfortunate friend Harriet," he writes under date August 15, 1811, from London, whether he had hurried to arrange the affairs of his elopement, "is yet undecided; not with respect to me, but to herself. How much, my dear friend, have I to tell you. In my leisure moments for thought, which since I wrote have been few, I have considered the important point on which you reprobated my hasty decision. The ties of love and honour are doubtless of sufficient strength to bind congenial souls—they are doubtless indissoluble, but by the brutish force of power; they are delicate and satisfactory. Yet the arguments of impracticability, and what is even worse, the disproportionate sacrifice which the female is called upon to make—these arguments, which you have urged in a manner immediately irresistible, I cannot withstand. Not that I suppose it to be likely that I shall directly be called upon to evince my attachment to either theory. I am become a perfect convert to matrimony, not from temporizing, but from YOUR arguments; nor, much as I wish to emulate your virtues and liken myself to you, do I regret the prejudices of anti-matrimonialism from your example or assertion. No. The ONE argument, which you have urged so often with so much energy; the sacrifice made by the woman, so disproportioned to any which the man can give—this alone may exculpate me, were it a fault, from uninquiring submission to your superior intellect."

Whether Shelley from his own peculiar point of view was morally justified in twice marrying, is a question of casuistry which has often haunted me. The reasons he alleged in extenuation of his conduct with regard to Harriet prove the goodness of his heart, his openness to argument, and the delicacy of his unselfishness. But they do not square with his expressed code of conduct; nor is it easy to understand how, having found it needful to submit to custom, for his partner's sake, he should have gone on denouncing an institution which he recognized in his own practice. The conclusion seems to be that, though he despised accepted usage, and would fain have fashioned the world afresh to suit his heart's desire, the instincts of a loyal gentleman and his practical good sense were stronger than his theories.

A letter from Shelley's cousin, Mr. C.H. Grove, gives the details of Harriet's elopement. "When Bysshe finally came to town to elope with Miss Westbrook, he came as usual to Lincoln's Inn Fields, and I was his companion on his visits to her, and finally accompanied them early one morning—I forget now the month, or the date, but it might have been September—in a hackney coach to the Green Dragon, in Gracechurch Street, where we remained all day, till the hour when the mail-coaches start, when they departed in the northern mail for York." From York the young couple made their way at once to Edinburgh, where they were married according to the formalities of the Scotch law.

Shelley had now committed that greatest of social crimes in his father's eyes—a mesalliance. Supplies and communications were at once cut off from the prodigal; and it appears that Harriet and he were mainly dependent upon the generosity of Captain Pilfold for subsistence. Even Jew Westbrook, much as he may have rejoiced at seeing his daughter wedded to the heir of several thousands a year, buttoned up his pockets, either because he thought it well to play the part of an injured parent, or because he was not certain about Shelley's expectations. He afterwards made the Shelleys an allowance of 200 pounds a year, and early in 1812 Shelley says that he is in receipt of twice that income. Whence we may conclude that both fathers before long relented to the extent of the sum above mentioned.

In spite of temporary impecuniosity, the young people lived happily enough in excellent lodgings in George Street. Hogg, who joined them early in September, has drawn a lively picture of their domesticity. Much of the day was spent in reading aloud; for Harriet, who had a fine voice and excellent lungs, was never happy unless she was allowed to read and comment on her favourite authors. Shelley sometimes fell asleep during the performance of these rites; but when he woke refreshed with slumber, he was no less ready than at Oxford to support philosophical paradoxes with impassioned and persuasive eloquence. He began to teach Harriet Latin, set her to work upon the translation of a French story by Madame Cottin, and for his own part executed a version of one of Buffon's treatises. The sitting-room was full of books. It was one of Shelley's peculiarities to buy books wherever he went, regardless of their volume or their cost. These he was wont to leave behind, when the moment arrived for a sudden departure from his temporary abode; so that, as Hogg remarks, a fine library might have been formed from the waifs and strays of his collections scattered over the three kingdoms. This quiet course of life was diversified by short rambles in the neighbourhood of Edinburgh, and by many episodes related with Hogg's caustic humour. On the whole, the impression left upon the reader's mind is that Shelley and Harriet were very happy together at this period, and that Harriet was a charming and sweet-tempered girl, somewhat too much given to the study of trite ethics, and slightly deficient in sensibility, but otherwise a fit and soothing companion for the poet.

They were not, however, content to remain in Edinburgh. Hogg was obliged to leave that city, in order to resume his law studies at York, and Shelley's programme of life at this period imperatively required the society of his chosen comrade. It was therefore decided that the three friends should settle at York, to remain "for ever" in each other's company. They started in a post-chaise, the good Harriet reading aloud novels by the now forgotten Holcroft with untiring energy, to charm the tedium of the journey. At York more than one cloud obscured their triune felicity. In the first place they were unfortunate in their choice of lodgings. In the second Shelley found himself obliged to take an expensive journey to London, in the fruitless attempt to come to some terms with his father's lawyer, Mr. Whitton. Mr. Timothy Shelley was anxious to bind his erratic son down to a settlement of the estates, which, on his own death, would pass into the poet's absolute control. He suggested numerous arrangements; and not long after the date of Shelley's residence in York, he proposed to make him an immediate allowance of 2000 pounds, if Shelley would but consent to entail the land on his heirs male. This offer was indignantly refused. Shelley recognized the truth that property is a trust far more than a possession, and would do nothing to tie up so much command over labour, such incalculable potentialities of social good or evil, for an unborn being of whose opinions he knew nothing. This is only one among many instances of his readiness to sacrifice ease, comfort, nay, the bare necessities of life, for principle.

On his return to York, Shelley found a new inmate established in their lodgings. The incomparable Eliza, who was henceforth doomed to guide his destinies to an obscure catastrophe, had arrived from London. Harriet believed her sister to be a paragon of beauty, good sense, and propriety. She obeyed her elder sister like a mother; never questioned her wisdom; and foolishly allowed her to interpose between herself and her husband. Hogg had been told before her first appearance in the friendly circle that Eliza was "beautiful, exquisitely beautiful; an elegant figure, full of grace; her face was lovely,—dark, bright eyes; jet-black hair, glossy; a crop upon which she bestowed the care it merited,—

almost all her time; and she was so sensible, so amiable, so good!" Now let us listen to the account he has himself transmitted of this woman, whom certainly he did not love, and to whom poor Shelley had afterwards but little reason to feel gratitude. "She was older than I had expected, and she looked much older than she was. The lovely face was seamed with the smallpox, and of a dead white, as faces so much marked and scarred commonly are; as white indeed as a mass of boiled rice, but of a dingy hue, like rice boiled in dirty water. The eyes were dark, but dull, and without meaning; the hair was black and glossy, but coarse; and there was the admired crop—a long crop, much like the tail of a horse—a switch tail. The fine figure was meagre, prim, and constrained. The beauty, the grace, and the elegance existed, no doubt, in their utmost perfection, but only in the imagination of her partial young sister. Her father, as Harriet told me, was familiarly called 'Jew Westbrook,' and Eliza greatly resembled one of the dark-eyed daughters of Judah."

This portrait is drawn, no doubt, with an unfriendly hand; and, in Hogg's biography, each of its sarcastic touches is sustained with merciless reiteration, whenever the mention of Eliza's name is necessary. We hear, moreover, how she taught the blooming Harriet to fancy that she was a victim of her nerves, how she checked her favourite studies, and how she ruled the household by continual reference to a Mrs. Grundy of her earlier experience. "What would Miss Warne say?" was as often on her lips, if we may credit Hogg, as the brush and comb were in her hands.

The intrusion of Eliza disturbed the harmony of Shelley's circle; but it is possible that there were deeper reasons for the abrupt departure which he made from York with his wife and her sister in November, 1811. One of his biographers asserts with categorical precision that Shelley had good cause to resent Hogg's undue familiarity with Harriet, and refers to a curious composition, published by Hogg as a continuation of Goethe's "Werther", but believed by Mr. McCarthy to have been a letter from the poet to his friend, in confirmation of his opinion. (McCarthy's Shelley's Early Life, page 117.) However this may be, the precipitation with which the Shelleys quitted York, scarcely giving Hogg notice of their resolution, is insufficiently accounted for in his biography.

The destination of the travellers was Keswick. Here they engaged lodgings for a time, and then moved into a furnished house. Probably Shelley was attracted to the lake country as much by the celebrated men who lived there, as by the beauty of its scenery, and the cheapness of its accommodation. He had long entertained an admiration for Southey's poetry, and was now beginning to study Wordsworth and Coleridge. But if he hoped for much companionship with the literary lions of the lakes, he was disappointed. Coleridge was absent, and missed making his acquaintance—a circumstance he afterwards regretted, saying that he could have been more useful to the young poet and metaphysician than Southey. De Quincey, though he writes ambiguously upon this point, does not seem to have met Shelley. Wordsworth paid him no attention; and though he saw a good deal of Southey, this intimacy changed Shelley's early liking for the man and poet into absolute contempt. It was not likely that the cold methodical student, the mechanical versifier, and the political turncoat, who had outlived all his earlier illusions, should retain the good-will of such an Ariel as Shelley, in whose brain "Queen Mab" was already simmering. Life at Keswick began to be monotonous. It was, however, enlivened by a visit to the Duke of Norfolk's seat, Greystoke. Shelley spent his last guinea on the trip; but though the ladies of his family enjoyed the honour of some days passed in ducal hospitalities, the visit was not fruitful of results. The Duke at this time kindly did his best, but without success, to bring about a reconciliation between his old friend, the member for Horsham, and his rebellious son.

Another important incident of the Keswick residence was Shelley's letter to William Godwin, whose work on Political Justice he had studied with unbounded admiration. He never spoke of this book without respect in after-life, affirming that the perusal of it had turned his attention from romances to questions of public utility. The earliest letter dated to Godwin from Keswick, January 3, 1812, is in many respects remarkable, and not the least so as a specimen of self-delineation. He entreats Godwin to become his guide, philosopher, and friend, urging that "if desire for universal happiness has any claim upon your preference," if persecution and injustice suffered in the cause of philanthropy and truth may commend a young man to William Godwin's regard, he is not unworthy of this honour. We who have learned to know the flawless purity of Shelley's aspirations, can refrain from smiling at the big generalities of this epistle. Words which to men made callous by long contact with the world, ring false and wake suspicion, were for Shelley but the natural expression of his most abiding mood. Yet Godwin may be pardoned if he wished to know more in detail of the youth, who sought to cast himself upon his care in all the panoply of phrases about philanthropy and universal happiness. Shelley's second letter contains an extraordinary mixture of truth willingly communicated, and of curious romance, illustrating his tendency to colour facts with the hallucinations of an ardent fancy. Of his sincerity there is, I think, no doubt. He really meant what he wrote; and yet we have no reason to believe the statement that he was twice expelled from Eton for disseminating the doctrines of "Political Justice", or that his father wished to drive him by poverty to accept a commission in some distant regiment, in order that he might prosecute the "Necessity of Atheism" in his absence, procure a sentence of outlawry, and so convey the family estates to his younger brother. The embroidery of bare fact with a tissue of imagination was a peculiarity of Shelley's mind; and this letter may be used as a key for the explanation of many strange occurrences in his biography. What he tells Godwin about his want of love for his father, and his inability to learn from the tutors imposed upon him at Eton and Oxford, represents the simple truth. Only from teachers chosen by himself, and recognized as his superiors by his own deliberate judgment, can he receive instruction. To Godwin he resigns himself with the implicit confidence of admiration. Godwin was greatly struck with this letter. Indeed, he must have been "or God or beast," like the insensible man in Aristotle's "Ethics", if he could have resisted the devotion of so splendid and high-spirited a nature, poured forth in language at once so vehement and so convincingly sincere. He accepted the responsible post of Shelley's Mentor; and thus began a connexion which proved not only a source of moral support and intellectual guidance to the poet, but was also destined to end in a closer personal tie between the two illustrious men.

In his second letter Shelley told Godwin that he was then engaged in writing "An inquiry into the causes of the failure of the French Revolution to benefit mankind," adding, "My plan is that of resolving to lose no opportunity to disseminate truth and happiness." Godwin sensibly replied that Shelley was too young to set himself up as a teacher and apostle: but his pupil did not take the hint. A third letter (January 16, 1812) contains this startling announcement: "In a few days we set off to Dublin. I do not know exactly where, but a letter addressed to Keswick will find me. Our journey has been settled some time. We go principally TO FORWARD AS MUCH AS WE CAN the Catholic Emancipation." In a fourth letter (January 28, 1812) he informs Godwin that he has already prepared an address to the Catholics of Ireland, and combats the dissuasions of his counsellor with ingenious arguments to prove that his contemplated expedition can do no harm, and may be fruitful of great good.

It appears that for some time past Shelley had devoted his attention to Irish politics. The persecution of Mr. Peter Finnerty, an Irish journalist and editor of "The Press" newspaper, who had been sentenced to eighteen months' imprisonment in Lincoln jail (between February 7, 1811, and August 7, 1812) for plain speech about Lord Castlereagh, roused his hottest indignation. He published a poem, as yet unrecovered, for his benefit; the proceeds of the sale amounting, it is said, to nearly one hundred pounds. (McCarthy, page 255.) The young enthusiast, who was attempting a philosophic study of the French Revolution, whose heart was glowing with universal philanthropy, and who burned to disseminate truth and happiness, judged that Ireland would be a fitting field for making a first experiment in practical politics. Armed with the manuscript of his "Address to the Irish People" (It was published in Dublin. See reprint in McCarthy, page 179.), he set sail with Harriet and Eliza on the 3rd of February from Whitehaven. They touched the Isle of Man; and after a very stormy passage, which drove them to the north coast of Ireland, and forced them to complete their journey by land, the party reached Dublin travel-worn, but with unabated spirit, on the 12th. Harriet shared her husband's philanthropical enthusiasm. "My wife," wrote Shelley to Godwin, "is the partner of my thoughts and feelings." Indeed, there is abundant proof in both his letters and hers, about this period, that they felt and worked together. Miss Westbrook, meantime, ruled the household; "Eliza keeps our common stock of money for safety in some nook or corner of her dress, but we are not dependent on her, although she gives it out as we want it." This master-touch of unconscious delineation tells us all we need to know about the domestic party now established in 7, Lower Sackville Street. Before a week had passed, the "Address to the Irish People" had been printed. Shelley and Harriet immediately engaged their whole energies in the task of distribution. It was advertised for sale; but that alone seemed insufficient. On the 27th of February Shelley wrote to a friend in England: "I have already sent 400 of my Irish pamphlets into the world, and they have excited a sensation of wonder in Dublin. Eleven hundred yet remain for distribution. Copies have been sent to sixty public houses.... Expectation is on the tiptoe. I send a man out every day to distribute copies, with instructions where and how to give them. His account corresponds with the multitudes of people who possess them. I stand at the balcony of our window and watch till I see a man WHO LOOKS LIKELY. I throw a book to him."

A postscript to this letter lets us see the propaganda from Harriet's point of view. "I am sure you would laugh were you to see us give the pamphlets. We throw them out of the window, and give them to men that we pass in the streets. For myself, I am ready to die of laughter when it is done, and Percy looks so grave. Yesterday he put one into a woman's hood of a cloak."

The purpose of this address was to rouse the Irish people to a sense of their real misery, to point out that Catholic Emancipation and a Repeal of the Union Act were the only radical remedies for their wrongs, and to teach them the spirit in which they should attempt a revolution. On the last point Shelley felt intensely. The whole address aims at the inculcation of a noble moral temper, tolerant, peaceful, resolute, rational, and self-denying. Considered as a treatise on the principles which should govern patriots during a great national crisis, the document is admirable: and if the inhabitants of Dublin had been a population of Shelleys, its effect might have been permanent and overwhelming. The mistake lay in supposing that a people whom the poet himself described as "of scarcely greater elevation in the scale of intellectual being than the oyster," were qualified to take the remedy of their grievances into their own hands, or were amenable to such sound reasoning as he poured forth. He told Godwin that he had "wilfully vulgarized the language of this pamphlet, in order to reduce the remarks it contains to the taste and comprehension of the Irish peasantry." A few extracts will enable the reader to judge how far he had succeeded in this aim. I select such as seem to me most valuable for the light they throw upon his own opinions. "All religions are good which make men good; and the way that a person ought to prove that his method of worshipping God is best, is for himself to be better than all other men." "A Protestant is my brother, and a Catholic is my brother." "Do not inquire if a man be a heretic, if he be a Quaker, a Jew, or a heathen; but if he be a virtuous man, if he loves liberty and truth, if he wish the happiness and peace of human kind. If a man be ever so much a believer and love not these things, he is a heartless hypocrite, a rascal and a knave." "It is not a merit to tolerate, but it is a crime to be intolerant." "Anything short of unlimited toleration and complete charity with all men, on which you will recollect that Jesus Christ principally insisted, is wrong." "Be calm, mild, deliberate, patient.... Think and talk and discuss.... Be free and be happy, but first be wise and good." Proceeding to recommend the formation of associations, he condemns secret and violent societies; "Be fair, open and you will be terrible to your enemies." "Habits of SOBRIETY, REGULARITY, and THOUGHT must be entered into and firmly resolved upon." Then follow precepts, which Shelley no doubt regarded as practical, for the purification of private morals, and the regulation of public discussion by the masses whom he elsewhere recognized as "thousands huddled together, one mass of animated filth."

The foregoing extracts show that Shelley was in no sense an inflammatory demagogue; however visionary may have been the hopes he indulged, he based those hopes upon the still more Utopian foundation of a sudden ethical reform, and preached a revolution without bloodshed. We find in them, moreover, the germs of "The Revolt of Islam", where the hero plays the part successfully in fiction, which the poet had attempted without appreciable result in practice at Dublin. The same principles guided Shelley at a still later period. When he wrote his "Masque of Anarchy", he bade the people of England to assemble by thousands, strong in the truth and justice of their cause, invincible in peaceful opposition to force.

While he was sowing his Address broadcast in the streets of Dublin, Shelley was engaged in printing a second pamphlet on the subject of Catholic Emancipation. It was entitled "Proposals for an Association", and advocated in serious and temperate phrase the formation of a vast society, binding all the Catholic patriots of Ireland together, for the recovery of their rights. In estimating Shelley's political sagacity, it must be remembered that Catholic emancipation has since his day been brought about by the very measure he proposed and under the conditions he foresaw. Speaking of the English Government in his Address, he used these simple phrases:—"It wants altering and mending. It will be mended, and a reform of English Government will produce good to the Irish." These sentences were prophetic; and perhaps they are destined to be even more so.

With a view to presenting at one glance Shelley's position as a practical politician, I shall anticipate the course of a few years, and compare his Irish pamphlets with an essay published in 1817, under the title of "A Proposal for putting Reform to the Vote throughout the Kingdom". He saw that the House of Commons did not represent the country; and acting upon his principle that government is the servant of the governed, he sought means for ascertaining the real will of the nation with regard to its Parliament, and for bringing the collective opinion of the population to bear upon its rulers. The plan proposed was that a huge network of committees should be formed, and that by their means every individual man should be canvassed. We find here the same method of advancing reform by peaceable associations as in Ireland. How moderated were his own opinions with regard to the franchise, is proved by the following sentence:—"With respect to Universal Suffrage, I confess I consider its adoption, in the present unprepared state of public knowledge and feeling, a measure fraught with peril. I think that none but those who register their names as paying a certain small sum in DIRECT TAXES ought at present to send members to Parliament." As in the case of Ireland, so in that of England, subsequent events have shown that Shelley's hopes were not exaggerated.

While the Shelleys were in Dublin, a meeting of the Irish Catholics was announced for the evening of February 28. It was held in Fishamble Street

Theatre; and here Shelley made his debut as an orator. He spoke for about an hour; and his speech was, on the whole, well received, though it raised some hisses at the beginning by his remarks upon Roman Catholicism. There is no proof that Shelley, though eloquent in conversation, was a powerful public speaker. The somewhat conflicting accounts we have received of this, his maiden effort, tend to the impression that he failed to carry his audience with him. The dissemination of his pamphlets had, however, raised considerable interest in his favour; and he was welcomed by the press as an Englishman of birth and fortune, who wished well to the Irish cause. His youth told somewhat against him. It was difficult to take the strong words of the beardless boy at their real value; and as though to aggravate this drawback, his Irish servant, Daniel Hill, an efficient agent in the dissemination of the Address, affirmed that his master was fifteen—four years less than his real age.

In Dublin Shelley made acquaintance with Curran, whose jokes and dirty stories he could not appreciate, and with a Mr. Lawless, who began a history of the Irish people in concert with the young philosopher. We also obtain, from one of Harriet's letters, a somewhat humorous peep at another of their friends, a patriotic Mrs. Nugent, who supported herself by working in a furrier's shop, and who is described as "sitting in the room now, and talking to Percy about Virtue." After less than two months' experience of his Irish propaganda, Shelley came to the conclusion that he "had done all that he could." The population of Dublin had not risen to the appeal of their Laon with the rapidity he hoped for; and accordingly upon the 7th of April he once more embarked with his family for Holyhead. In after-days he used to hint that the police had given him warning that it would be well for him to leave Dublin; but, though the danger of a prosecution was not wholly visionary, this intimation does not seem to have been made. Before he quitted Ireland, however, he despatched a box containing the remaining copies of his "Address" and "Proposals", together with the recently printed edition of another manifesto, called a "Declaration of Rights", to a friend in Sussex. This box was delayed at the Holyhead custom-house, and opened. Its contents gave serious anxiety to the Surveyor of Customs, who communicated the astonishing discovery through the proper official channels to the government. After some correspondence, the authorities decided to take no steps against Shelley, and the box was forwarded to its destination.

The friend in question was a Miss Eliza Hitchener, of Hurstpierpoint, who kept a sort of school, and who had attracted Shelley's favourable notice by her advanced political and religious opinions. He does not seem to have made her personal acquaintance; but some of his most interesting letters from Ireland are addressed to her. How recklessly he entered into serious entanglements with people whom he had not learned to know, may be gathered from these extracts:—"We will meet you in Wales, and never part again. It will not do. In compliance with Harriet's earnest solicitations, I entreated you instantly to come and join our circle, resign your school, all, everything for us and the Irish cause." "I ought to count myself a favoured mortal with such a wife and such a friend." Harriet addressed this lady as "Portia;" and it is an undoubted fact that soon after their return to England, Miss Hitchener formed one of their permanent family circle. Her entrance into it and her exit from it at no very distant period are, however, both obscure. Before long she acquired another name than Portia in the Shelley household, and now she is better known as the "Brown Demon." Eliza Westbrook took a strong dislike to her; Harriet followed suit; and Shelley himself found that he had liked her better at a distance than in close companionship. She had at last to be bought off or bribed to leave.

The scene now shifts with bewildering frequency; nor is it easy to trace the Shelleys in their rapid flight. About the 21st of April, they settled for a short time at Nantgwilt, near Rhayader, in North Wales. Ere long we find them at Lynmouth, on the Somersetshire coast. Here Shelley continued his political propaganda, by circulating the "Declaration of Rights", whereof mention has already been made. It was, as Mr. W.M. Rossetti first pointed out, a manifesto concerning the ends of government and the rights of man,—framed in imitation of two similar French Revolutionary documents, issued by the Constituent Assembly in August, 1789, and by Robespierre in April, 1793. (Reprinted in McCarthy, page 324.) Shelley used to seal this pamphlet in bottles and set it afloat upon the sea, hoping perhaps that after this wise it would traverse St. George's Channel and reach the sacred soil of Erin. He also employed his servant, Daniel Hill, to distribute it among the Somersetshire farmers. On the 19th of August this man was arrested in the streets of Barnstaple, and sentenced to six months' imprisonment for uttering a seditious pamphlet; and the remaining copies of the "Declaration of Rights" were destroyed. In strong contrast with the puerility of these proceedings, is the grave and lofty "Letter to Lord Ellenborough", composed at Lynmouth, and printed at Barnstaple. (Reprinted in Lady Shelley's Memorials, page 29.) A printer, named D.J. Eaton, had recently been sentenced to imprisonment by his Lordship for publishing the Third Part of Paine's "Age of Reason". Shelley's epistle is an eloquent argument in favour of toleration and the freedom of the intellect, carrying the matter beyond the instance of legal tyranny which occasioned its composition, and treating it with philosophic, if impassioned seriousness.

An extract from this composition will serve to show his power of handling weighty English prose, while yet a youth of hardly twenty. I have chosen a passage bearing on his theological opinions:—

"Moral qualities are such as only a human being can possess. To attribute them to the Spirit of the Universe, or to suppose that it is capable of altering them, is to degrade God into man, and to annex to this incomprehensible Being qualities incompatible with any possible definition of his nature.

"It may be here objected: Ought not the Creator to possess the perfections of the creature? No. To attribute to God the moral qualities of man, is to suppose him susceptible of passions, which, arising out of corporeal organization, it is plain that a pure spirit cannot possess.... But even suppose, with the vulgar, that God is a venerable old man, seated on a throne of clouds, his breast the theatre of various passions, analogous to those of humanity, his will changeable and uncertain as that of an earthly king; still, goodness and justice are qualities seldom nominally denied him, and it will be admitted that he disapproves of any action incompatible with those qualities. Persecution for opinion is unjust. With what consistency, then, can the worshippers of a Deity whose benevolence they boast, embitter the existence of their fellow-being, because his ideas of that Deity are different from those which they entertain? Alas! there is no consistency in those persecutors who worship a benevolent Deity; those who worship a demon would alone act consonantantly to these principles by imprisoning and torturing in his name."

Shelley had more than once urged Godwin and his family to visit him. The sage of Skinner Street thought that now was a convenient season. Accordingly he left London, and travelled by coach to Lynmouth, where he found that the Shelleys had flitted a few days previously without giving any notice. This fruitless journey of the poet's Mentor is humorously described by Hogg, as well as one undertaken by himself in the following year to Dublin with a similar result. The Shelleys were now established at Tan-yr-allt, near Tremadoc, in North Wales, on an estate belonging to Mr. W.A. Madocks, M.P. for Boston. This gentleman had reclaimed a considerable extent of marshy ground from the sea, and protected it with an embankment. Shelley, whose interest in the poor people around him was always keen and practical, lost no time in making their acquaintance at Tremadoc. The work of utility carried out by his landlord aroused his enthusiastic admiration; and when the embankment was emperilled by a heavy sea, he got up a subscription for its preservation. Heading the list with 500 pounds, how raised, or whether paid, we know not, he endeavoured to extract similar sums from the neighbouring gentry, and even ran up with Harriet to London to use his influence for the same purpose with the Duke of Norfolk. On this occasion he made the personal acquaintance of the Godwin family.

Life at Tanyrallt was smooth and studious, except for the diversion caused by the peril to the embankment. We hear of Harriet continuing her Latin studies, reading Odes of Horace, and projecting an epistle in that language to Hogg. Shelley, as usual, collected many books around him. There are letters extant in which he writes to London for Spinoza and Kant, Plato, and the works of the chief Greek historians. It appears that at this period, under the influence of Godwin, he attempted to conquer a strong natural dislike of history. "I am determined to apply myself to a study which is hateful and disgusting to my very soul, but which is above all studies necessary for him who would be listened to as a mender of antiquated abuses,—I mean, that record of crimes and miseries—history." Although he may have made an effort to apply himself to historical reading, he was not successful. His true bias inclined him to metaphysics coloured by a glowing fancy, and to poetry penetrated with speculative enthusiasm. In the historic sense he was deficient; and when he made a serious effort at a later period to compose a tragedy upon the death of Charles I, this work was taken up with reluctance, continued with effort, and finally abandoned.

In the same letters he speaks about a collection of short poems on which he was engaged, and makes frequent allusions to "Queen Mab". It appears, from his own assertion, and from Medwin's biography, that a poem on Queen Mab had been projected and partially written by him at the early age of eighteen. But it was not taken seriously in hand until the spring of 1812; nor was it finished and printed before 1813. The first impression was a private issue of 250 copies, on fine paper, which Shelley distributed to people whom he wished to influence. It was pirated soon after its appearance, and again in 1821 it was given to the public by a bookseller named Clarke. Against the latter republication Shelley energetically protested, disclaiming in a letter addressed to "The Examiner", from Pisa, June 22, 1821, any interest in a production which he had not even seen for several years. "I doubt not but that it is perfectly worthless in point of literary composition; and that in all that concerns moral and political speculation, as well as in the subtler discriminations of metaphysical and religious doctrine, it is still more crude and immature. I am a devoted enemy to religious, political and domestic oppression; and I regret this publication, not so much from literary vanity as because I fear it is better fitted to injure than to serve the sacred cause of freedom." This judgment is undoubtedly severe; but, though exaggerated in its condemnation, it, like all Shelley's criticisms on his own works, expresses the truth. We cannot include "Queen Mab", in spite of its sonorous rhetoric and fervid declamation, in the canon of his masterpieces. It had a succes de scandale on its first appearance, and fatally injured Shelley's reputation. As a work of art it lacks maturity and permanent vitality.

The Shelleys were suddenly driven away from Tanyrallt by a mysterious occurrence, of which no satisfactory explanation has yet been given. According to letters written by himself and Harriet soon after the event, and confirmed by the testimony of Eliza, Shelley was twice attacked upon the night of February 24 by an armed ruffian, with whom he struggled in hand-to-hand combat. Pistols were fired and windows broken, and Shelley's nightgown was shot through: but the assassin made his escape from the house without being recognized. His motive and his personality still remain matters of conjecture. Whether the whole affair was a figment of Shelley's brain, rendered more than usually susceptible by laudanum taken to assuage intense physical pain; whether it was a perilous hoax played upon him by the Irish servant, Daniel Hill; or whether, as he himself surmised, the crime was instigated by an unfriendly neighbour, it is impossible to say. Strange adventures of this kind, blending fact and fancy in a now inextricable tangle, are of no unfrequent occurrence in Shelley's biography. In estimating the relative proportions of the two factors in this case, it must be borne in mind, on the one hand, that no one but Shelley, who was alone in the parlour, and who for some unexplained reason had loaded his pistols on the evening before the alleged assault, professed to have seen the villain; and, on the other, that the details furnished by Harriet, and confirmed at a subsequent period by so hostile a witness as Eliza, are too circumstantial to be lightly set aside.

On the whole it appears most probable that Shelley on this night was the subject of a powerful hallucination. The theory of his enemies at Tanyrallt, that the story had been invented to facilitate his escape from the neighbourhood without paying his bills, may be dismissed. But no investigation on the spot could throw any clear light on the circumstance, and Shelley's friends, Hogg, Peacock, and Mr. Madocks, concurred in regarding the affair as a delusion.

There was no money in the common purse of the Shelleys at this moment. In their distress they applied to Mr. T. Hookham, a London publisher, who sent them enough to carry them across the Irish channel. After a short residence in 35, Cuffe Street, Dublin, and a flying visit to Killarney, they returned to London. Eliza, for some reason as unexplained as the whole episode of this second visit to Ireland, was left behind for a short season. The flight from Tanyrallt closes the first important period of Shelley's life; and his settlement in London marks the beginning of another, fruitful of the gravest consequences and decisive of his future.

CHAPTER 4

SECOND RESIDENCE IN LONDON, AND
SEPARATION FROM HARRIET

EARLY in May the Shelleys arrived in London, where they were soon joined by Eliza, from whose increasingly irksome companionship the poet had recently enjoyed a few weeks' respite. After living for a short while in hotels, they took lodgings in Half Moon Street. The house had a projecting window, where the poet loved to sit with book in hand, and catch, according to his custom, the maximum of sunlight granted by a chary English summer. "He wanted," said one of his female admirers, "only a pan of clear water and a fresh turf to look like some young lady's lark, hanging outside for air and song." According to Hogg, this period of London life was a pleasant and tranquil episode in Shelley's troubled career. His room was full of books, among which works of German metaphysics occupied a prominent place, though they were not deeply studied. He was now learning Italian, and made his first acquaintance with Tasso, Ariosto, and Petrarch.

The habits of the household were, to say the least, irregular; for Shelley took no thought of sublunary matters, and Harriet was an indifferent housekeeper. Dinner seems to have come to them less by forethought than by the operation of divine chance; and when there was no meat provided for the entertainment of casual guests, the table was supplied with buns, procured by Shelley from the nearest pastry-cook. He had already abjured animal food and alcohol; and his favourite diet consisted of pulse or bread, which he ate dry with water, or made into panada. Hogg relates how, when he was walking in the streets and felt hungry, he would dive into a baker's shop and emerge with a loaf tucked under his arm. $This he consumed as he went along, very often reading at the same time, and dodging the foot-passengers with the rapidity of movement which distinguished him. He could not comprehend how any man should want more than bread. "I have dropped a word, a hint," says Hogg, "about a pudding; a pudding, Bysshe said dogmatically, is a prejudice." This indifference to diet was highly characteristic of Shelley. During the last years of his life, even when he was suffering from the frequent attacks of a painful disorder, he took no heed of food; and his friend, Trelawny, attributes the derangement of his health, in a great measure, to this carelessness. Mrs. Shelley used to send him something to eat into the room where he habitually studied; but the plate frequently remained untouched for hours upon a bookshelf, and at the end of the day he might be heard asking, "Mary, have I dined?" His dress was no less simple than his diet. Hogg says that he never saw him in a great coat, and that his collar was unbuttoned to let the air play freely on his throat. "In the street or road he reluctantly wore a hat; but in fields and gardens, his little round head had no other covering than his long, wild, ragged locks." Shelley's head, as is well known, was remarkably small and round; he used to plunge it several times a day in cold water, and expose it recklessly to the intensest heat of fire or sun. Mrs.

Shelley relates that a great part of the "Cenci" was written on their house-roof near Leghorn, where Shelley lay exposed to the unmitigated ardour of Italian summer heat; and Hogg describes him reading Homer by a blazing fire-light, or roasting his skull upon the hearth-rug by the hour.

These personal details cannot be omitted by the biographer of such a man as Shelley. He was an elemental and primeval creature, as little subject to the laws of custom in his habits as in his modes of thought, living literally as the spirit moved him, with a natural nonchalance that has perhaps been never surpassed. To time and place he was equally indifferent, and could not be got to remember his engagements. "He took strange caprices, unfounded frights and dislikes, vain apprehensions and panic terrors, and therefore he absented himself from formal and sacred engagements. He was unconscious and oblivious of times, places, persons and seasons; and falling into some poetic vision, some day-dream, he quickly and completely forgot all that he had repeatedly and solemnly promised; or he ran away after some object of imaginary urgency and importance, which suddenly came into his head, setting off in vain pursuit of it, he knew not whither. When he was caught, brought up in custody, and turned over to the ladies, with, Behold, your King! to be caressed, courted, admired, and flattered, the king of beauty and fancy would too commonly bolt; slip away, steal out, creep off; unobserved and almost magically he vanished; thus mysteriously depriving his fair subjects of his much-coveted, long looked-for company." If he had been fairly caged and found himself in congenial company, he let time pass unheeded, sitting up all night to talk, and chaining his audience by the spell of his unrivalled eloquence; for wonderful as was his poetry, those who enjoyed the privilege of converse with him, judged it even more attractive. "He was commonly most communicative, unreserved, and eloquent, and enthusiastic, when those around him were inclining to yield to the influence of sleep, or rather at the hour when they would have been disposed to seek their chambers, but for the bewitching charms of his discourse."

From Half Moon Street the Shelleys moved into a house in Pimlico; and it was here, according to Hogg, or at Cooke's Hotel in Dover Street according to other accounts, that Shelley's first child, Ianthe Eliza, was born about the end of June, 1813. Harriet did not take much to her little girl, and gave her over to a wet-nurse, for whom Shelley conceived a great dislike. That a mother should not nurse her own baby was no doubt contrary to his principles; and the double presence of the servant and Eliza, whom he now most cordially detested, made his home uncomfortable. We have it on excellent authority, that of Mr. Peacock, that he "was extremely fond of it (the child), and would walk up and down a room with it in his arms for a long time together, singing to it a song of his own making, which ran on the repetition of a word of his own coining. His song was Yáhmani, Yáhmani, Yáhmani, Yáhmani." To the want of sympathy between the father and the mother in this matter of Ianthe, Mr. Peacock is inclined to attribute the beginning of troubles in the Shelley household. There is, indeed, no doubt that the revelation of Harriet's maternal coldness must have been extremely painful to her husband; and how far she carried her insensibility, may be gathered from a story told by Hogg about her conduct during an operation performed upon the child.

During this period of his sojourn in London, Shelley was again in some pecuniary difficulties. Yet he indulged Harriet's vanity by setting up a carriage, in which they afterwards took a hurried journey to Edinburgh and back. He narrowly escaped a debtor's prison through this act of extravagance, and by a somewhat ludicrous mistake Hogg was arrested for the debt due to the coach-maker. His acquaintances were few and scattered, and he saw nothing of his family. Gradually, however, he seems to have become a kind of prophet in a coterie of learned ladies. The views he had propounded in "Queen Mab", his passionate belief in the perfectibility of man, his vegetarian doctrines, and his readiness to adopt any new nostrum for the amelioration of his race, endeared him to all manners of strange people; nor was he deterred by aristocratic prejudices from frequenting society which proved extremely uncongenial to Hogg, and of which we have accordingly some caustic sketches from his pen. His chief friends were a Mrs. Boinville, for whom he conceived an enthusiastic admiration, and her daughter Cornelia, married to a vegetarian, Mr. Newton. In order to be near them he had moved to Pimlico; and his next move, from London to a cottage named High Elms, at Bracknell, in Berkshire, had the same object. With Godwin and his family he was also on terms of familiar intercourse. Under the philosopher's roof in Skinner Street there was now gathered a group of miscellaneous inmates—Fanny Imlay, the daughter of his first wife, Mary Wollstonecraft; Mary, his own daughter by the same marriage; his second wife, and her two children, Claire and Charles Clairmont, the offspring of a previous union. From this connexion with the Godwin household events of the gravest importance in the future were destined to arise, and already it appears that Fanny Imlay had begun to look with perilous approval on the fascinating poet. Hogg and Mr. Peacock, the well-known novelist, described by Mrs. Newton as "a cold scholar, who, I think, has neither taste nor feeling," were his only intimates.

Mrs. Newton's unfair judgment of Mr. Peacock marks a discord between the two chief elements of Shelley's present society; and indeed it will appear to a careful student of his biography that Hogg, Peacock, and Harriet, now stood somewhat by themselves and aloof from the inner circle of his associates. If we regard the Shelleys as the centre of an extended line, we shall find the Westbrook family at one end, the Boinville family at the other, with Hogg and Peacock somewhere in the middle. Harriet was naturally drawn to the Westbrook extremity, and Shelley to the Boinville. Peacock had no affinity for either, but a sincere regard for Harriet as well as for her husband; while Hogg was in much the same position, except that he had made friends with Mrs. Newton. The Godwins, of great importance to Shelley himself, exercised their influence at a distance from the rest. Frequent change from Bracknell to London and back again, varied by the flying journey to Edinburgh, and a last visit paid in strictest secrecy to his mother and sisters, at Field Place, of which a very interesting record is left in the narrative of Mr. Kennedy, occupied the interval between July, 1813, and March, 1814. The period was not productive of literary masterpieces. We only hear of a "Refutation of Deism", a dialogue between Eusebes and Theosophus, which attacked all forms of Theistic belief.

Since we are now approaching the gravest crisis in Shelley's life, it behoves us to be more than usually careful in considering his circumstances at this epoch. His home had become cold and dull. Harriet did not love her child, and spent her time in a great measure with her Mount Street relations. Eliza was a source of continual irritation, and the Westbrook family did its best, by interference and suggestion, to refrigerate the poet's feelings for his wife. On the other hand he found among the Boinville set exactly that high-flown, enthusiastic, sentimental atmosphere which suited his idealizing temper. Two extracts from a letter written to Hogg upon the 16th of March, 1814, speak more eloquently than any analysis, and will place before the reader the antagonism which had sprung up in Shelley's mind between his own home and the circle of his new friends:—"I have been staying with Mrs. B— for the last month; I have escaped, in the society of all that philosophy and friendship combine, from the dismaying solitude of myself. They have revived in my heart the expiring flame of life. I have felt myself translated to a paradise, which has nothing of mortality but its transitoriness; my heart sickens at the view of that necessity, which will quickly divide me from the delightful tranquillity of this happy home,—for it has become my home. The trees, the bridge, the minutest objects, have already a place in my affections."

"Eliza is still with us—not here!—but will be with me when the infinite malice of destiny forces me to depart. I am now but little inclined to contest this point. I certainly hate her with all my heart and soul. It is a sight which awakens an inexpressible sensation of disgust and horror, to see her caress my poor little Ianthe, in whom I may hereafter find the consolation of sympathy. I sometimes feel faint with the fatigue of checking the overflowings of my unbounded abhorrence for this miserable wretch. But she is no more than a blind and loathsome worm, that cannot see to sting."

While divided in this way between a home which had become distasteful to him, and a house where he found scope for his most romantic outpourings of sensibility, Shelley fell suddenly and passionately in love with Godwin's daughter, Mary. Peacock, who lived in close intimacy with him at this period, must deliver his testimony as to the overwhelming nature of the new attachment:—"Nothing that I ever read in tale or history could present a more striking image of a sudden, violent, irresistible, uncontrollable passion, than that under which I found him labouring when, at his request, I went up from the country to call on him in London. Between his old feelings towards Harriet, FROM WHOM HE WAS NOT THEN SEPARATED, and his new passion for Mary, he showed in his looks, in his gestures, in his speech, the state of a mind 'suffering, like a little kingdom, the nature of an insurrection.' His eyes were bloodshot, his hair and dress disordered. He caught up a bottle of laudanum, and said, 'I never part from this.'"

We may therefore affirm, I think, with confidence that in the winter and spring of 1814, Shelley had been becoming gradually more and more estranged from Harriet, whose commonplace nature was no mate for his, and whom he had never loved with all the depth of his affection; that his intimacy with the Boinville family had brought into painful prominence whatever was jarring and repugnant to him in his home; and that in this crisis of his fate he had fallen in love for the first time seriously with Mary Godwin. (The date at which he first made Mary's acquaintance is uncertain. Peacock says that it was between April 18 and June 8.) She was then a girl of sixteen, "fair and fair-haired, pale indeed, and with a piercing look," to quote Hogg's description of her, as she first appeared before him on the 8th or 9th of June, 1814. With her freedom from prejudice, her tense and high-wrought sensibility, her acute intellect, enthusiasm for ideas, and vivid imagination, Mary Godwin was naturally a fitter companion for Shelley than the good Harriet, however beautiful.

That Shelley early in 1814 had no intention of leaving his wife, is probable; for he was re-married to her on the 24th of March, eight days after his impassioned letter to Hogg, in St. George's, Hanover Square. Harriet was pregnant, and this ratification of the Scotch marriage was no doubt intended to place the legitimacy of a possible heir beyond all question. Yet it seems, if we may found conjecture on "Stanzas, April, 1814," that in the very month after this new ceremony Shelley found the difficulties of his wedded life insuperable, and that he was already making up his mind to part from Harriet. About the middle of June the separation actually occurred—not by mutual consent, so far as any published documents throw light on the matter, but rather by Shelley's sudden abandonment of his wife and child. (Leigh Hunt, Autobiography page 236, and Medwin, however, both assert that it was by mutual consent. The whole question must be studied in Peacock and in Garnett, Relics of Shelly, page 147.) For a short while Harriet was left in ignorance of his abode, and with a very insufficient sum of money at her disposal. She placed herself under the protection of her father, retired to Bath, and about the beginning of July received a letter from Shelley, who was thenceforth solicitous for her welfare, keeping up a correspondence with her, supplying her with funds, and by no means shrinking from personal communications.

That Shelley must bear the responsibility of this separation seems to me quite clear. His justification is to be found in his avowed opinions on the subject of love and marriage—opinions which Harriet knew well and professed to share, and of which he had recently made ample confession in the notes to "Queen Mab". The world will still agree with Lord Eldon in regarding those opinions as dangerous to society, and a blot upon the poet's character; but it would be unfair, while condemning them as frankly as he professed them, to blame him also because he did not conform to the opposite code of morals, for which he frequently expressed extreme abhorrence, and which he stigmatized, however wrongly, as the source of the worst social vices. It must be added that the Shelley family in their memorials of the poet, and through their friend, Mr. Richard Garnett, inform us, without casting any slur on Harriet, that documents are extant which will completely vindicate the poet's conduct in this matter. It is therefore but just to await their publication before pronouncing a decided judgment. Meanwhile there remains no doubt about the fact that forty days after leaving Harriet, Shelley departed from London with Mary Godwin, who had consented to share his fortunes. How he plighted his new troth, and won the hand of her who was destined to be his companion for life, may best be told in Lady Shelley's words:—

"His anguish, his isolation, his difference from other men, his gifts of genius and eloquent enthusiasm, made a deep impression on Godwin's daughter Mary, now a girl of sixteen, who had been accustomed to hear Shelley spoken of as something rare and strange. To her, as they met one eventful day in St. Pancras Churchyard, by her mother's grave, Bysshe, in burning words, poured forth the tale of his wild past—how he had suffered, how he had been misled, and how, if supported by her love, he hoped in future years to enrol his name with the wise and good who had done battle for the fellow-men, and been true through all adverse storms to the cause of humanity. Unhesitatingly, she placed her hand in his, and linked her fortune with his own; and most truthfully, as the remaining portions of these Memorials will prove, was the pledge of both redeemed. The theories in which the daughter of the authors of "Political Justice", and of the "Rights of Woman", had been educated, spared her from any conflict between her duty and her affection. For she was the child of parents whose writings had had for their object to prove that marriage was one among the many institutions which a new era in the history of mankind was about to sweep away. By her father, whom she loved—by the writings of her mother, whom she had been taught to venerate—these doctrines had been rendered familiar to her mind. It was therefore natural that she should listen to the dictates of her own heart, and willingly unite her fate with one who was so worthy of her love."

Soon after her withdrawal to Bath, Harriet gave birth to Shelley's second child, Charles Bysshe, who died in 1826. She subsequently formed another connexion which proved unhappy; and on the 10th of November, 1816, she committed suicide by drowning herself in the Serpentine. The distance of time between June, 1814, and November, 1816, and the new ties formed by Harriet in this interval, prove that there was no immediate connexion between Shelley's abandonment of his wife and her suicide. She had always entertained the thought of self-destruction, as Hogg, who is no adverse witness in her case, has amply recorded; and it may be permitted us to suppose that, finding herself for the second time unhappy in her love, she reverted to a long-since cherished scheme, and cut the knot of life and all its troubles.

So far as this is possible, I have attempted to narrate the most painful period in Shelley's life as it occurred, without extenuation and without condemnation. Until the papers, mentioned with such insistence by Lady Shelley and Mr. Garnett, are given to the world, it is impossible that the poet should not bear the reproach of heartlessness and inconstancy in this the gravest of all human relations. Such, however, is my belief in the essential goodness of his character, after allowing, as we must do, for the operation of his peculiar principles upon his conduct, that I for my own part am willing to suspend my judgment till the time arrives for his vindication. The language used by Lady Shelley and Mr.

Garnett justify us in expecting that that vindication will be as startling as complete. If it is not, they, as pleading for him, will have overshot the mark of prudence.

On the 28th of July Shelley left London with Mary Godwin, who up to this date had remained beneath her father's roof. There was some secrecy in their departure, because they were accompanied by Miss Clairmont, whose mother disapproved of her forming a third in the party. Having made their way to Dover, they crossed the Channel in an open boat, and went at once to Paris. Here they hired a donkey for their luggage, intending to perform the journey across France on foot. Shelley, however, sprained his ancle, and a mule-carriage was provided for the party. In this conveyance they reached the Jura, and entered Switzerland at Neufchatel. Brunnen, on the Lake of Lucerne, was chosen for their residence; and here Shelley began his romantic tale of "The Assassins", a portion of which is printed in his prose works. Want of money compelled them soon to think of turning their steps homeward; and the back journey was performed upon the Reuss and Rhine. They reached Gravesend, after a bad passage, on the 13th of September. Mrs. Shelley's "History of a Six Week's Tour" relates the details of this trip, which was of great importance in forming Shelley's taste, and in supplying him with the scenery of river, rock, and mountain, so splendidly utilized in "Alastor".

The autumn was a period of more than usual money difficulty; but on the 6th of January, 1815, Sir Bysshe died, Percy became the next heir to the baronetcy and the family estates, and an arrangement was made with his father by right of which he received an allowance of 1000 pounds a year. A portion of his income was immediately set apart for Harriet. The winter was passed in London, where Shelley walked a hospital, in order, it is said, to acquire some medical knowledge that might be of service to the poor he visited. His own health at this period was very bad. A physician whom he consulted pronounced that he was rapidly sinking under pulmonary disease, and he suffered frequent attacks of acute pain. The consumptive symptoms seem to have been so marked that for the next three years he had no doubt that he was destined to an early death. In 1818, however, all danger of phthisis passed away; and during the rest of his short life he only suffered from spasms and violent pains in the side, which baffled the physicians, but, though they caused him extreme anguish, did not menace any vital organ. To the subject of his health it will be necessary to return at a later period of this biography. For the present it is enough to remember that his physical condition was such as to justify his own expectation of death at no distant time. (See Letter to Godwin in Shelley's Memorials, page 78.)

Fond as ever of wandering, Shelley set out in the early summer for a tour with Mary. They visited Devonshire and Clifton, and then settled in a house on Bishopsgate Heath, near Windsor Forest. The summer was further broken by a water excursion up the Thames to its source, in the company of Mr. Peacock and Charles Clairmont. Peacock traces the poet's taste for boating, which afterwards became a passion with him, to this excursion. About this there is, however, some doubt. Medwin tells us that Shelley while a boy delighted in being on the water, and that he enjoyed the pastime at Eton. On the other hand, Mr. W.S. Halliday, a far better authority than Medwin, asserts positively that he never saw Shelley on the river at Eton, and Hogg relates nothing to prove that he practised rowing at Oxford. It is certain that, though inordinately fond of boats and every kind of water—river, sea, lake, or canal—he never learned to swim. Peacock also notices his habit of floating paper boats, and gives an amusing description of the boredom suffered by Hogg on occasions when Shelley would stop by the side of a pond or mere to float a mimic navy. The not altogether apocryphal story of his having once constructed a boat out of a bank-post-bill, and launched it on the lake in Kensington Gardens, deserves to be alluded to in this connexion.

On their return from this river journey, Shelley began the poem of "Alastor", haunting the woodland glades and oak groves of Windsor Forest, and drawing from that noble scenery his inspiration. It was printed with a few other poems in one volume the next year. Not only was "Alastor" the first serious poem published by Shelley; but it was also the first of his compositions which revealed the greatness of his genius. Rarely has blank verse been written with more majesty and music; and while the influence of Milton and Wordsworth may be traced in certain passages, the versification, tremulous with lyrical vibrations, is such as only Shelley could have produced.

"Alastor" is the Greek name for a vengeful daemon, driving its victim into desert places; and Shelley, prompted by Peacock, chose it for the title of a poem which describes the Nemesis of solitary souls. Apart from its intrinsic merit as a work of art, "Alastor" has great autobiographical value. Mrs. Shelley affirms that it was written under the expectation of speedy death, and under the sense of disappointment, consequent upon the misfortunes of his early life. This accounts for the somewhat unhealthy vein of sentiment which threads the wilderness of its sublime descriptions. All that Shelley had observed of natural beauty—in Wales, at Lynton, in Switzerland, upon the eddies of the Reuss, beneath the oak shades of the forest—is presented to us in a series of pictures penetrated with profound emotion. But the deeper meaning of "Alastor" is to be found, not in the thought of death nor in the poet's recent communings with nature, but in the motto from St. Augustine placed upon its title page, and in the "Hymn to Intellectual Beauty", composed about a year later. Enamoured of ideal loveliness, the poet pursues his vision through the universe, vainly hoping to assuage the thirst which has been stimulated in his spirit, and vainly longing for some mortal realization of his love. "Alastor", like "Epipsychidion," reveals the mistake which Shelley made in thinking that the idea of beauty could become incarnate for him in any earthly form: while the "Hymn to Intellectual Beauty" recognizes the truth that such realization of the ideal is impossible. The very last letter written by Shelley sets the misconception in its proper light: "I think one is always in love with something or other; the error, and I confess it is not easy for spirits cased in flesh and blood to avoid it, consists in seeking in a mortal image the likeness of what is, perhaps, eternal." But this Shelley discovered only with "the years that bring the philosophic mind," and when he was upon the very verge of his untimely death.

The following quotation is a fair specimen of the blank verse of "Alastor". It expresses that longing for perfect sympathy in an ideal love, which the sense of divine beauty had stirred in the poet's heart:—

> At length upon the lone Chorasmian shore
> He paused, a wide and melancholy waste
> Of putrid marshes. A strong impulse urged
> His steps to the sea-shore. A swan was there,
> Beside a sluggish stream among the reeds.
> It rose as he approached, and, with strong wings
> Scaling the upward sky, bent its bright course
> High over the immeasurable main.
> His eyes pursued its flight:—"Thou hast a home,
> Beautiful bird! thou voyagest to thine home,
> Where thy sweet mate will twine her downy neck
> With thine, and welcome thy return with eyes
> Bright in the lustre of their own fond joy.
> And what am I that I should linger here,
> With voice far sweeter than thy dying notes,
> Spirit more vast than thine, frame more attuned
> To beauty, wasting these surpassing powers
> In the deaf air, to the blind earth, and heaven
> That echoes not my thoughts?" A gloomy smile
> Of desperate hope wrinkled his quivering lips.
> For Sleep, he knew, kept most relentlessly
> Its precious charge, and silent Death exposed,
> Faithless perhaps as Sleep, a shadowy lure,
> With doubtful smile mocking its own strange charms.

William, the eldest son of Shelley and Mary Godwin, was born on the 24th of January, 1816. In the spring of that year they went together, accompanied by Miss Clairmont, for a second time to Switzerland. They reached Geneva on the 17th of May and were soon after joined by Lord Byron and his travelling physician, Dr. Polidori. Shelley had not yet made Byron's acquaintance, though he had sent him a copy of "Queen Mab", with a letter, which miscarried in the post. They were now thrown into daily intercourse, occupying the villas Diodati and Mount Alegre, at no great distance from each other, passing their days upon the lake in a boat which they purchased, and spending the nights in conversation. Miss Clairmont had known Byron in London, and their acquaintance now ripened into an intimacy, the fruit of which was the child Allegra. This fact has to be mentioned by Shelley's biographer, because Allegra afterwards became an inmate of his home; and though he and Mary were ignorant of what was passing at Geneva, they did not withdraw their sympathy from the mother of Lord Byron's daughter. The lives of Byron and Shelley during the next six years were destined to be curiously blent. Both were to seek in Italy an exile-home; while their friendship was to become one of the most interesting facts of English literary history. The influence of Byron upon Shelley, as he more than once acknowledged, and as his wife plainly perceived, was, to a great extent, depressing. For Byron's genius and its fruits in poetry he entertained the highest possible opinion. He could not help comparing his own achievement and his fame with Byron's; and the result was that in the presence of one whom he erroneously believed to be the greater poet, he became inactive. Shelley, on the contrary, stimulated Byron's productive faculty to nobler efforts, raised his moral tone, and infused into his less subtle intellect something of his own philosophical depth and earnestness. Much as he enjoyed Byron's society and admired his writing, Shelley was not blind to the imperfections of his nature. The sketch which he has left us of Count Maddalo, the letters written to his wife from Venice and Ravenna, and his correspondence on the subject of Leigh Hunt's visit to Italy, supply the most discriminating criticism which has yet been passed upon his brother poet's character. It is clear that he never found in Byron a perfect friend, and that he had not accepted him as one with whom he sympathized upon the deeper questions of feeling and conduct. Byron, for his part, recognized in Shelley the purest nature he had ever known. "He was the most gentle, the most amiable, and least worldly-minded person I ever met; full of delicacy, disinterested beyond all other men, and possessing a degree of genius joined to simplicity as rare as it is admirable. He had formed to himself a beau ideal of all that is fine, high-minded, and noble, and he acted up to this ideal even to the very letter."

Toward the end of June the two poets made the tour of Lake Geneva in their boat, and were very nearly wrecked off the rocks of Meillerie. On this occasion Shelley was in imminent danger of death from drowning. His one anxiety, however, as he wrote to Peacock, was lest Byron should attempt to save him at the risk of his own life. Byron described him as "bold as a lion;" and indeed it may here be said, once and for all, that Shelley's physical courage was only equalled by his moral fearlessness. He carried both without bravado to the verge of temerity, and may justly be said to have never known what terror was. Another summer excursion was a visit to Chamouni, of which he has left memorable descriptions in his letters to Peacock, and in the somewhat Coleridgian verses on Mont Blanc. The preface to "Laon and Cythna" shows what a powerful impression had been made upon him by the glaciers, and how he delighted in the element of peril. There is a tone of exultation in the words which record the experiences of his two journeys in Switzerland and France:—"I have been familiar from boyhood with mountains and lakes and the sea, and the solitude of forests. Danger, which sports upon the brink of precipices, has been my playmate. I have trodden the glaciers of the Alps, and lived under the eye of Mont Blanc. I have been a wanderer among distant fields. I have sailed down mighty rivers, and seen the sun rise and set, and the stars come forth, whilst I have sailed night and day down a rapid stream among mountains. I have seen populous cities, and have watched the passions which rise and spread, and sink and change amongst assembled multitudes of men. I have seen the theatre of the more visible ravages of tyranny and war, cities and villages reduced to scattered groups of black and roofless houses, and the naked inhabitants sitting famished upon their desolated thresholds."

On their return to the lake, the Shelleys found M.G. Lewis established with Byron. This addition to the circle introduced much conversation about apparitions, and each member of the party undertook to produce a ghost story. Polidori's "Vampyre" and Mrs. Shelley's "Frankenstein" were the only durable results of their determination. But an incident occurred which is of some importance in the history of Shelley's psychological condition. Toward midnight on the 18th of July, Byron recited the lines in "Christabel" about the lady's breast; when Shelley suddenly started up, shrieked, and fled from the room. He had seen a vision of a woman with eyes instead of nipples. At this time he was writing notes upon the phenomena of sleep to be inserted in his "Speculations on Metaphysics", and Mrs. Shelley informs us that the mere effort to remember dreams of thrilling or mysterious import so disturbed his nervous system that he had to relinquish the task. At no period of his life was he wholly free from visions which had the reality of facts. Sometimes they occurred in sleep, and were prolonged with painful vividness into his waking moments. Sometimes they seemed to grow out of his intense meditation, or to present themselves before his eyes as the projection of a powerful inner impression. All his sensations were abnormally acute, and his ever-active imagination confused the border-lands of the actual and the visionary. Such a nature as Shelley's, through its far greater susceptibility than is common even when with artistic temperaments, was debarred in moments of high-strung emotion from observing the ordinary distinctions of subject and object; and this peculiar quality must never be forgotten when we seek to estimate the proper proportions of Dichtung and Wahreit in certain episodes of his biography. The strange story, for example, told by Peacock about a supposed warning he had received in the spring of this year from Mr. Williams of Tremadoc, may possibly be explained on the hypothesis that his brooding thoughts had taken form before him, both ear and eye having been unconsciously pressed into the service of a subjective energy. (Fraser's Magazine, January, 1860, page 98.)

On their return to England in September, Shelley took a cottage at Great Marlow on the Thames, in order to be near his friend Peacock. While it was being prepared for the reception of his family, he stayed at Bath, and there heard of Harriet's suicide. The life that once was dearest to him, had ended thus in misery, desertion, want. The mother of his two children, abandoned by both her husband and her lover, and driven from her father's home, had drowned herself after a brief struggle with circumstance. However Shelley may have felt that his conscience was free from blame, however small an element of self-reproach may have mingled with his grief and horror, there is no doubt that he suffered most acutely. His deepest ground for remorse seems to have been the conviction that he had drawn Harriet into a sphere of thought and feeling for which she was not qualified, and that had it not been for him and his opinions, she might have lived a happy woman in some common walk of life. One of his biographers asserts that "he continued to be haunted by certain recollections, partly real and partly imaginative, which pursued him like an Orestes," and even Trelawny, who knew him only in the last months of his life, said that the impression of that dreadful moment was still vivid. We may trace the echo of his feelings in some painfully pathetic verses written in 1817 (Forman, 3 148.); and though he did not often speak of Harriet, Peacock has recorded one memorable occasion on which he disclosed the anguish of his spirit to a friend. (Fraser, January, 1860, page 102.)

Shelley hurried at once to London, and found some consolation in the society of Leigh Hunt. The friendship extended to him by that excellent man at this season of his trouble may perhaps count for something with those who are inclined to judge him harshly. Two important events followed immediately upon the tragedy. The first was Shelley's marriage with Mary Godwin on the 30th of December, 1816. Whether Shelley would have taken this step except under strong pressure from without, appears to me very doubtful. Of all men who ever lived, he was the most resolutely bent on confirming his theories by his practice; and in this instance there was no valid reason why he should not act up to principles professed in common by himself and the partner of his fortunes, no less than by her father and mother. It is, therefore, reasonable to suppose that he yielded to arguments; and these arguments must have been urged by Godwin, who had never treated him with cordiality since he left England in 1816. Godwin, though overrated in his generation, and almost ludicrously idealized by Shelley, was a man whose talents verged on genius. But he was by no means consistent. His conduct in money-matters shows that he could not live the life of a self-sufficing philosopher; while the irritation he expressed when Shelley omitted to address him as Esquire, stood in comic contradiction with his published doctrines. We are therefore perhaps justified in concluding that he worried Shelley, the one enthusiastic and thorough-going follower he had, into marrying his daughter in spite of his disciple's protestations; nor shall we be far wrong if we surmise that Godwin congratulated himself on Mary's having won the right to bear the name of a future baronet.

The second event was the refusal of Mr. Westbrook to deliver up the custody of his grandchildren. A chancery suit was instituted; at the conclusion of which, in August, 1817, Lord Eldon deprived Shelley of his son and daughter on the double ground of his opinions expressed in "Queen Mab", and of his conduct toward his first wife. The children were placed in the hands of a clergyman, to be educated in accordance with principles diametrically opposed to their parent's, while Shelley's income was mulcted in a sum of 200 pounds for their maintenance. Thus sternly did the father learn the value of that ancient Aeschylean maxim, to drasanti pathein, the doer of the deed must suffer. His own impulsiveness, his reckless assumption of the heaviest responsibilities, his overweening confidence in his own strength to move the weight of the world's opinions, had brought him to this tragic pass—to the suicide of the woman who had loved him, and to the sequestration of the offspring whom he loved.

Shelley is too great to serve as text for any sermon; and yet we may learn from him as from a hero of Hebrew or Hellenic story. His life was a tragedy; and like some protagonist of Greek drama, he was capable of erring and of suffering greatly. He had kicked against the altar of justice as established in the daily sanctities of human life; and now he had to bear the penalty. The conventions he despised and treated like the dust beneath his feet, were found in this most cruel crisis to be a rock on which his very heart was broken. From this rude trial of his moral nature he arose a stronger being; and if longer life had been granted him, he would undoubtedly have presented the ennobling spectacle of one who had been lessoned by his own audacity, and by its bitter fruits, into harmony with the immutable laws which he was ever seeking to obey. It is just this conflict between the innate rectitude of Shelley's over-daring nature and the circumstances of ordinary existence, which makes his history so tragic; and we may justly wonder whether, when he read the Sophoclean tragedies of Oedipus, he did not apply their doctrine of self-will and Nemesis to his own fortunes.

CHAPTER 5

LIFE AT MARLOW, AND JOURNEY TO ITALY

AMID the torturing distractions of the Chancery suit about his children, and the still more poignant anguish of his own heart, and with the cloud of what he thought swift-coming death above his head, Shelley worked steadily, during the summer of 1817, upon his poem of "Laon and Cythna". Six months were spent in this task. "The poem," to borrow Mrs. Shelley's words, "was written in his boat, as it floated under the beech-groves of Bisham, or during wanderings in the neighbouring country, which is distinguished for peculiar beauty." Whenever Shelley could, he composed in the open air. The terraces of the Villa Cappuccini at Este and the Baths of Caracalla were the birthplace of "Prometheus". "The Cenci" was written on the roof of the Villa Valsovano at Leghorn. The Cascine of Florence, the pine-woods near Pisa, the lawns above San Guiliano, and the summits of the Euganean Hills, witnessed the creation of his loveliest lyrics; and his last great poem, the "Triumph of Life", was transferred to paper in his boat upon the Bay of Spezia.

If "Alastor" had expressed one side of Shelley's nature, his devotion to Ideal Beauty, "Laon and Cythna" was in a far profounder sense representative of its author. All his previous experiences and all his aspirations—his passionate belief in friendship, his principle of the equality of women with men, his demand for bloodless revolution, his confidence in eloquence and reason to move nations, his doctrine of free love, his vegetarianism, his hatred of religious intolerance and tyranny—are blent together and concentrated in the glowing cantos of this wonderful romance. The hero, Laon, is himself idealized, the self which he imagined when he undertook his Irish campaign. The heroine, Cythna, is the helpmate he had always dreamed, the woman exquisitely feminine, yet capable of being fired with male enthusiasms, and of grappling the real problems of our nature with a man's firm grasp. In the first edition of the poem he made Laon and Cythna brother and sister, not because he believed in the desirability of incest, but because he wished to throw a glove down to society, and to attack the intolerance of custom in its stronghold. In the preface, he tells us that it was his purpose to kindle in the bosoms of his readers "a virtuous enthusiasm for those doctrines of liberty and justice, that faith and hope in something good, which neither violence nor misrepresentation, nor prejudice, can ever wholly extinguish among mankind;" to illustrate "the growth and progress of individual mind aspiring after excellence, and devoted to the love of mankind;" and to celebrate Love "as the sole law which should govern the moral world." The wild romantic treatment of this didactic motive makes the poem highly characteristic of its author. It is written in Spenserian stanzas, with a rapidity of movement and a dazzling brilliance that are Shelley's own. The story relates the kindling of a nation to freedom at the cry of a young poet-prophet, the temporary triumph of the good cause, the final victory of despotic force, and the martyrdom of the hero, together with whom the heroine falls a willing victim. It is full of thrilling incidents and lovely pictures; yet the tale is the least part of the poem; and few readers have probably been able either to sympathize with its visionary characters, or to follow the narrative without weariness. As in the case of other poems by Shelley—especially those in which he attempted to tell a story, for which kind of art his genius was not well suited—the central motive of "Laon and Cythna" is surrounded by so radiant a photosphere of imagery and eloquence that it is difficult to fix our gaze upon it, blinded as we are by the excess of splendour. Yet no one now can read the terrible tenth canto, or the lovely fifth, without feeling that a young eagle of poetry had here tried the full strength of his pinions in their flight. This truth was by no means recognized when "Laon and Cythna" first appeared before the public. Hooted down, derided, stigmatized, and howled at, it only served to intensify the prejudice with which the author of "Queen Mab" had come to be regarded.

I have spoken of this poem under its first name of "Laon and Cythna". A certain number of copies were issued with this title (How many copies were put in circulation is not known. There must certainly have been many more than the traditional three; for when I was a boy at Harrow, I picked up two uncut copies in boards at a Bristol bookshop, for the price of 2 shillings and 6 pence a piece.); but the publisher, Ollier, not without reason dreaded the effect the book would make; he therefore induced Shelley to alter the relationship between the hero and his bride, and issued the old sheets with certain cancelled pages under the title of "Revolt of Islam". It was published in January, 1818. While still resident at Marlow, Shelley began two autobiographical poems—the one "Prince Athanase," which he abandoned as too introspective and morbidly self-analytical, the other, "Rosalind and Helen", which he finished afterwards in Italy. Of the second of these compositions he entertained a poor opinion; nor will it bear comparison with his best work. To his biographer its chief interest consists in the character of Lionel, drawn less perhaps exactly from himself than as an ideal of the man he would have wished to be. The poet in "Alastor", Laon in the "Revolt of Islam", Lionel in "Rosalind and Helen", and Prince Athanase, are in fact a remarkable row of self-portraits, varying in the tone and scale of idealistic treatment bestowed upon them. Later on in life, Shelley outgrew this preoccupation with his idealized self, and directed his genius to more objective themes. Yet the autobiographic tendency, as befitted a poet of the highest lyric type, remained to the end a powerful characteristic.

Before quitting the first period of Shelley's development, it may be well to set before the reader a specimen of that self-delineative poetry which characterized it; and since it is difficult to detach a single passage from the continuous stanzas of "Laon and Cythna", I have chosen the lines in "Rosalind and Helen" which describe young Lionel:

> To Lionel,
> Though of great wealth and lineage high,
> Yet through those dungeon walls there came
> Thy thrilling light, O Liberty!

And as the meteor's midnight flame
Startles the dreamer, sun-like truth
Flashed on his visionary youth,
And filled him, not with love, but faith.
And hope, and courage mute in death;
For love and life in him were twins,
Born at one birth: in every other
First life, then love its course begins,
Though they be children of one mother;
And so through this dark world they fleet
Divided, till in death they meet:
But he loved all things ever. Then
He past amid the strife of men,
And stood at the throne of armed power
Pleading for a world of woe:
Secure as one on a rock-built tower
O'er the wrecks which the surge trails to and fro,
'Mid the passions wild of human kind
He stood, like a spirit calming them;
For, it was said, his words could find
Like music the lulled crowd, and stem
That torrent of unquiet dream,
Which mortals truth and reason deem,
But IS revenge and fear and pride.
Joyous he was; and hope and peace
On all who heard him did abide,
Raining like dew from his sweet talk,
As where the evening star may walk
Along the brink of the gloomy seas,
Liquid mists of splendour quiver.
His very gestures touch'd to tears
The unpersuaded tyrant, never
So moved before: his presence stung
The torturers with their victim's pain,
And none knew how; and through their ears,
The subtle witchcraft of his tongue
Unlocked the hearts of those who keep
Gold, the world's bond of slavery.
Men wondered, and some sneer'd to see
One sow what he could never reap:
For he is rich, they said, and young,
And might drink from the depths of luxury.
If he seeks Fame, Fame never crown'd
The champion of a trampled creed:
If he seeks Power, Power is enthroned

'Mid ancient rights and wrongs, to feed
Which hungry wolves with praise and spoil,
Those who would sit near Power must toil;
And such, there sitting, all may see.

During the year he spent at Marlow, Shelley was a frequent visitor at Leigh Hunt's Hampstead house, where he made acquaintance with Keats, and the brothers Smith, authors of "Rejected Addresses". Hunt's recollections supply some interesting details, which, since Hogg and Peacock fail us at this period, may be profitably used. Describing the manner of his life at Marlow, Hunt writes as follows: "He rose early in the morning, walked and read before breakfast, took that meal sparingly, wrote and studied the greater part of the morning, walked and read again, dined on vegetables (for he took neither meat nor wine), conversed with his friends (to whom his house was ever open) again walked out, and usually finished with reading to his wife till ten o'clock, when he went to bed. This was his daily existence. His book was generally Plato, or Homer, or one of the Greek tragedians, or the Bible, in which last he took a great, though peculiar, and often admiring interest. One of his favourite parts was the book of Job." Mrs. Shelley, in her note on the "Revolt of Islam", confirms this account of his Bible studies; and indeed the influence of the Old Testament upon his style may be traced in several of his poems. In the same paragraph from which I have just quoted, Leigh Hunt gives a just notion of his relation to Christianity, pointing out that he drew a distinction between the Pauline presentation of the Christian creeds, and the spirit of the Gospels. "His want of faith in the letter, and his exceeding faith in the spirit of Christianity, formed a comment, the one on the other, very formidable to those who chose to forget what Scripture itself observes on that point." We have only to read Shelley's "Essay on Christianity", in order to perceive what reverent admiration he felt for Jesus, and how profoundly he understood the true character of his teaching. That work, brief as it is, forms one of the most valuable extant contributions to a sound theology, and is morally far in advance of the opinions expressed by many who regard themselves as specially qualified to speak on the subject. It is certain that, as Christianity passes beyond its mediaeval phase, and casts aside the husk of outworn dogmas, it will more and more approximate to Shelley's exposition. Here and here only is a vital faith, adapted to the conditions of modern thought, indestructible because essential, and fitted to unite instead of separating minds of divers quality. It may sound paradoxical to claim for Shelley of all men a clear insight into the enduring element of the Christian creed; but it was precisely his detachment from all its accidents which enabled him to discern its spiritual purity, and placed him in a true relation to its Founder. For those who would neither on the one hand relinquish what is permanent in religion, nor yet on the other deny the inevitable conclusions of modern thought, his teaching is indubitably valuable. His fierce tirades against historic Christianity must be taken as directed against an ecclesiastical system of spiritual tyranny, hypocrisy, and superstition, which in his opinion had retarded the growth of free institutions, and fettered the human intellect. Like, Campanella, he distinguished between Christ, who sealed the gospel of charity with his blood, and those Christians, who would be the first to crucify their Lord if he returned to earth.

That Shelley lived up to his religious creed is amply proved. To help the needy and to relieve the sick, seemed to him a simple duty, which he cheerfully discharged. "His charity, though liberal, was not weak. He inquired personally into the circumstances of his petitioners, visited the sick in their beds,....and kept a regular list of industrious poor, whom he assisted with small sums to make up their accounts." At Marlow, the miserable condition of the lace-makers called forth all his energies; and Mrs. Shelley tells us that an acute ophthalmia, from which he twice suffered, was contracted in a visit to their cottages. A story told by Leigh Hunt about his finding a woman ill on Hampstead Heath, and carrying her from door to door in the vain hopes of meeting with a man as charitable as himself, until he had to house the poor creature with his friends the Hunts, reads like a practical illustration of Christ's parable about the Good Samaritan. Nor was it merely to the so-called poor that Shelley showed his generosity. His purse was always open to his friends. Peacock received from him an annual allowance of 100 pounds. He gave Leigh Hunt, on one occasion, 1400 pounds; and he discharged debts of Godwin, amounting, it is said, to about 6000 pounds. In his pamphlet on "Putting Reform to the Vote", he offered to subscribe 100 pounds for the purpose of founding an association; and we have already seen that he headed the Tremadoc subscription with a sum of 500 pounds. These instances of his generosity might be easily multiplied; and when we remember that his present income was 1000 pounds, out of which 200 pounds went to the support of his children, it will be understood not only that he could not live luxuriously, but also that he was in frequent money difficulties through the necessity of raising funds upon his expectations. His self-denial in all minor matters of expenditure was conspicuous. Without a murmur, without ostentation, this heir of the richest baronet in Sussex illustrated by his own conduct those principles of democratic simplicity and of fraternal charity which formed his political and social creed.

A glimpse into the cottage at Great Marlow is afforded by a careless sentence of Leigh Hunt's. "He used to sit in a study adorned with casts, as large as life, of the Vatican Apollo and the celestial Venus." Fancy Shelley with his bright eyes and elf-locks in a tiny, low-roofed room, correcting proofs of "Laon and Cythna", between the Apollo of the Belvedere and Venus de' Medici, life-sized, and as crude as casts by Shout could make them! In this house, Miss Clairmont, with her brother and Allegra, lived as Shelley's guests; and here Clara Shelley was born on the 3rd of September, 1817. In the same autumn, Shelley suffered from a severe pulmonary attack. The critical state of his health, and the apprehension, vouched for by Mrs. Shelley, that the Chancellor might lay his vulture's talons on the children of his second marriage, were the motives which induced him to leave England for Italy in the spring of 1818. (See Note on Poems of 1819, and compare the lyric "The billows on the beach.") He never returned. Four years only of life were left to him—years filled with music that will sound as long as English lasts.

It was on the 11th of March that the Shelleys took their departure with Miss Clairmont and the child Allegra. They went straight to Milan, and after visiting the Lake of Como, Pisa, the Bagni di Lucca, Venice and Rome, they settled early in the following December at Naples. Shelley's letters to Peacock form the invaluable record of this period of his existence. Taken altogether, they are the most perfect specimens of descriptive prose in the English language; never over-charged with colour, vibrating with emotions excited by the stimulating scenes of Italy, frank in their criticism, and exquisitely delicate in observation. Their transparent sincerity and unpremeditated grace, combined with natural finish of expression, make them masterpieces of a style at once familiar and elevated. That Shelley's sensibility to art was not so highly cultivated as his feeling for nature, is clear enough in many passages: but there is no trace of admiring to order in his comments upon pictures or statues. Familiarity with the great works of antique and Italian art would doubtless have altered some of the opinions he at first expressed; just as longer residence among the people made him modify his views about their character. Meanwhile, the spirit of modest and unprejudiced attention in which he began his studies of sculpture and painting, might well be imitated in the present day by travellers who think that to pin their faith to some famous critic's verdict is the acme of good taste. If there were space for a long quotation from these letters, I should choose the description of Pompeii (January 26, 1819), or that of the Baths of Caracalla (March 23, 1819). As it is, I must content myself with a short but eminently characteristic passage, written from Ferrarra, November 7, 1818:—

"The handwriting of Ariosto is a small, firm, and pointed character, expressing, as I should say, a strong and keen, but circumscribed energy of mind; that of Tasso is large, free, and flowing, except that there is a checked expression in the midst of its flow, which brings the letters into a smaller compass than one expected from the beginning of the word. It is the symbol of an intense and earnest mind, exceeding at times its own depth, and admonished to return by the chillness of the waters of oblivion striking upon its adventurous feet. You know I always seek in what I see the manifestation of something beyond the present and tangible object; and as we do not agree in physiognomy, so we may not agree now. But my business is to relate my own sensations, and not to attempt to inspire others with them."

In the middle of August, Shelley left his wife at the Bagni di Lucca, and paid a visit to Lord Byron at Venice. He arrived at midnight in a thunderstorm. "Julian and Maddalo" was the literary fruit of this excursion—a poem which has rightly been characterized by Mr. Rossetti as the most perfect specimen in our language of the "poetical treatment of ordinary things." The description of a Venetian sunset, touched to sadness amid all its splendour by the gloomy presence of the madhouse, ranks among Shelley's finest word-paintings; while the glimpse of Byron's life is interesting on a lower level. Here is the picture of the sunset and the island of San Lazzaro:—

Oh!
How beautiful is sunset, when the glow
Of heaven descends upon a land like thee,
Thou paradise of exiles, Italy,
Thy mountains, seas, and vineyards, and the towers
Of cities they encircle!—it was ours
To stand on thee, beholding it: and then,
Just where we had dismounted, the Count's men
Were waiting for us with the gondola.
As those who pause on some delightful way,
Though bent on pleasant pilgrimage, we stood
Looking upon the evening, and the flood
Which lay between the city and the shore,
Paved with the image of the sky. The hoar
And airy Alps, towards the north, appeared,
Thro' mist, a heaven-sustaining bulwark, reared
Between the east and west; and half the sky
Was roofed with clouds of rich emblazonry,
Dark purple at the zenith, which still grew
Down the steep west into a wondrous hue
Brighter than burning gold, even to the rent
Where the swift sun yet paused in his descent
Among the many-folded hills. They were
Those famous Euganean hills, which bear,
As seem from Lido through the harbour piles,
The likeness of a clump of peaked isles—
And then, as if the earth and sea had been
Dissolved into one lake of fire, were seen
Those mountains towering, as from waves of flame,
Around the vaporous sun, from which there came
The inmost purple spirit of light, and made
Their very peaks transparent. "Ere it fade,"
Said my companion, "I will show you soon
A better station." So o'er the lagune
We glided; and from that funereal bark
I leaned, and saw the city, and could mark
How from their many isles, in evening's gleam,
Its temples and its palaces did seem
Like fabrics of enchantment piled to heaven.
I was about to speak, when—"We are even
Now at the point I meant," said Maddalo,
And bade the gondolieri cease to row.
"Look, Julian, on the west, and listen well
If you hear not a deep and heavy bell."
I looked, and saw between us and the sun

A building on an island, such a one
As age to age might add, for uses vile,—
A windowless, deformed, and dreary pile;
And on the top an open tower, where hung
A bell, which in the radiance swayed and swung,—
We could just hear its coarse and iron tongue:
The broad sun sank behind it, and it tolled
In strong and black relief—"What we behold
Shall be the madhouse and its belfry tower,"—
Said Maddalo; "and ever at this hour,
Those who may cross the water hear that bell,
Which calls the maniacs, each one from his cell,
To vespers."

It may be parenthetically observed that one of the few familiar quotations from Shelley's poems occurs in "Julian and Maddalo":—

Most wretched men
Are cradled into poetry by wrong:
They learn in suffering what they teach in song.

Byron lent the Shelleys his villa of the Cappuccini near Este, where they spent some weeks in the autumn. Here "Prometheus Unbound" was begun, and the "Lines written among the Euganean Hills" were composed; and here Clara became so ill that her parents thought it necessary to rush for medical assistance to Venice. They had forgotten their passport; but Shelley's irresistible energy overcame all difficulties, and they entered Venice—only in time, however, for the child to die.

Nearly the whole of the winter was spent in Naples, where Shelley suffered from depression of more than ordinary depth. Mrs. Shelley attributed this gloom to the state of his health, but Medwin tells a strange story, which, if it is not wholly a romance, may better account for the poet's melancholy. He says that so far back as the year 1816, on the night before his departure from London, "a married lady, young, handsome, and of noble connexions," came to him, avowed the passionate love she had conceived for him, and proposed that they should fly together. (Medwin's Life of Shelley, volume 1 324. His date, 1814, appears from the context to be a misprint.) He explained to her that his hand and heart had both been given irrevocably to another, and, after the expression of the most exalted sentiments on both sides, they parted. She followed him, however, from place to place; and without intruding herself upon his notice, found some consolation in remaining near him. Now she arrived at Naples; and at Naples she died. The web of Shelley's life was a wide one, and included more destinies than his own. Godwin, as we have reason to believe, attributed the suicide of Fanny Imlay to her hopeless love for Shelley; and the tale of Harriet has already been told. Therefore there is nothing absolutely improbable in

Medwin's story, especially when we remember what Hogg half-humorously tells us about Shelley's attraction for women in London. At any rate, the excessive wretchedness of the lyrics written at Naples can hardly be accounted for by the "constant and poignant physical sufferings" of which Mrs. Shelley speaks, since these were habitual with him. She was herself, moreover under the impression that he was concealing something from her, and we know from her own words in another place that his "fear to wound the feelings of others" often impelled him to keep his deepest sorrows to himself. (Note on the Revolt of Islam.)

All this while his health was steadily improving. The menace of consumption was removed; and though he suffered from severe attacks of pain in the side, the cause of this persistent malady does not seem to have been ascertained. At Naples he was under treatment for disease of the liver. Afterwards, his symptoms were ascribed to nephritis, and it is certain that his greater or less freedom from uneasiness varied with the quality of the water he drank. He was, for instance, forced to eschew the drinking water of Ravenna, because it aggravated his symptoms; while Florence, for a similar reason, proved an unsuitable residence. The final settlement of the Shelleys at Pisa seems to have been determined by the fact that the water of that place agreed with him. That the spasms which from time to time attacked him were extremely serious, is abundantly proved by the testimony of those who lived with him at this period, and by his own letters. Some relief was obtained by mesmerism, a remedy suggested by Medwin; but the obstinacy of the torment preyed upon his spirits to such an extent, that even during the last months of his life we find him begging Trelawny to procure him prussic acid as a final and effectual remedy for all the ills that flesh is heir to. It may be added that mental application increased the mischief, for he told Leigh Hunt that the composition of "The Cenci" had cost him a fresh seizure. Yet though his sufferings were indubitably real, the eminent physician, Vacca, could discover no organic disease; and possibly Trelawny came near the truth when he attributed Shelley's spasms to insufficient and irregular diet, and to a continual over-taxing of his nervous system.

Mrs. Shelley states that the change from England to Italy was in all respects beneficial to her husband. She was inclined to refer the depression from which he occasionally suffered, to his solitary habits; and there are several passages in his own letters which connect his melancholy with solitude. It is obvious that when he found himself in the congenial company of Trelawny, Williams, Medwin, or the Gisbornes, he was simply happy; and nothing could be further from the truth than to paint him as habitually sunk in gloom. On the contrary, we hear quite as much about his high spirits, his "Homeric laughter," his playfulness with children, his readiness to join in the amusements of his chosen circle, and his incomparable conversation, as we do about his solitary broodings, and the seasons when pain or bitter memories over-cast his heaven. Byron, who had some right to express a judgment in such a matter, described him as the most companionable man under the age of thirty he had ever met with. Shelley rode and practised pistol-shooting with his brother bard, sat up late to talk with him, enjoyed his jokes, and even betted with him on one occasion marked by questionable taste. All this is quite incompatible with that martyrdom to persecution, remorse, or physical suffering, with which it has pleased some romantic persons to invest the poet. Society of the ordinary kind he hated. The voice of a stranger, or a ring at the house-bell, heard from afar with Shelley's almost inconceivable quickness of perception, was enough to make him leave the house; and one of his prettiest poems is written on his mistaking his wife's mention of the Aziola, a little owl common enough in Tuscany, for an allusion to a tiresome visitor. This dislike for intercourse with commonplace people was a source of some disagreement between him and Mrs. Shelley, and kept him further apart from Byron than he might otherwise have been. In a valuable letter recently published by Mr. Garnett, he writes:—"I detest all society—almost all, at least—and Lord Byron is the nucleus of all that is hateful and tiresome in it." And again, speaking about his wife to Trelawny, he said:—"She can't bear solitude, nor I society—the quick coupled with the dead."

In the year 1818-19 the Shelleys had no friends at all in Italy, except Lord Byron at Venice, and Mr. and Mrs. John Gisborne at Leghorn. Mrs. Gisborne had been a friend of Mary Wollstonecraft and Godwin. She was a woman of much cultivation, devoid of prejudice, and, though less enthusiastic than Shelley liked, quite capable of appreciating the inestimable privilege of his acquaintance. Her husband, to use a now almost obsolete phrase, was a scholar and a gentleman. He shared his wife's enlightened opinions, and remained staunch through good and ill report to his new friends. At Rome and Naples they knew absolutely no one. Shelley's time was therefore passed in study and composition. In the previous summer he had translated the "Symposium" of Plato, and begun an essay on the Ethics of the Greeks, which remains unluckily a fragment. Together with Mary he read much Italian literature, and his observations on the chief Italian poets form a valuable contribution to their criticism. While he admired the splendour and invention of Ariosto, he could not tolerate his moral tone. Tasso struck him as cold and artificial, in spite of his "delicate moral sensibility." Boccaccio he preferred to both; and his remarks on this prose-poet are extremely characteristic. "How much do I admire Boccaccio! What descriptions of nature are those in his little introductions to every new day! It is the morning of life stripped of that mist of familiarity which makes it obscure to us. Boccaccio seems to me to have possessed a deep sense of the fair ideal of human life, considered in its social relations. His more serious theories of love agree especially with mine. He often expresses things lightly too, which have serious meanings of a very beautiful kind. He is a moral casuist, the opposite of the Christian, stoical, ready-made, and worldly system of morals. Do you remember one little remark, or rather maxim of his, which might do some good to the common, narrow-minded conceptions of love,—'Bocca baciata non perde ventura; anzi rinnouva, come fa la luna'?" Dante and Petrarch remained the objects of his lasting admiration, though the cruel Christianity of the "Inferno" seemed to him an ineradicable blot upon the greatest of Italian poems. Of Petrarch's "tender and solemn enthusiasm," he speaks with the sympathy of one who understood the inner mysteries of idealizing love.

It will be gathered from the foregoing quotations that Shelley, notwithstanding is profound study of style and his exquisite perception of beauty in form and rhythm, required more than merely artistic excellences in poetry. He judged poems by their content and spirit; and while he plainly expressed his abhorrence of the didactic manner, he held that art must be moralized in order to be truly great. The distinction he drew between Theocritus and the earlier Greek singers in the "Defence of Poetry", his severe strictures on "The Two Noble Kinsmen" in a letter to Mary (August 20, 1818) and his phrase about Ariosto, "who is entertaining and graceful, and SOMETIMES a poet," illustrate the application of critical canons wholly at variance with the "art for art" doctrine.

While studying Italian, he continued faithful to Greek. Plato was often in his hands, and the dramatists formed his almost inseparable companions. How deeply he felt the art of the Homeric poems, may be gathered from the following extract:—"I congratulate you on your conquest of the Iliad. You must have been astonished at the perpetually increasing magnificence of the last seven books. Homer there truly begins to be himself. The battle of the Scamander, the funeral of Patroclus, and the high and solemn close of the whole bloody tale in tenderness and inexpiable sorrow, are wrought in a manner incomparable with anything of the same kind. The Odyssey is sweet, but there is nothing like this." About this time, prompted by Mrs. Gisborne, he began the study of Spanish, and conceived an ardent admiration for Calderon, whose splendid and supernatural fancy tallied with his own. "I am bathing myself in the light and odour of the starry Autos," he writes to Mr. Gisborne in the autumn of 1820. "Faust", too, was a favourite. "I have been reading over and over again "Faust", and always with sensations which no other composition excites. It deepens the gloom and augments the rapidity of ideas, and would therefore seem to me an unfit study for any person who is a prey to the reproaches of memory, and the delusions of an imagination not to be restrained." The profound impression made upon him by Margaret's story is expressed in two letters about Retzsch's illustrations:—"The artist makes one envy his happiness that he can sketch such things with calmness, which I only dared look upon once, and which made my brain swim round only to touch the leaf on the opposite side of which I knew that it was figured."

The fruits of this occupation with Greek, Italian, Spanish, and German were Shelley's translations from Homer and Euripides, from Dante, from Calderon's "Magico Prodigioso", and from "Faust", translations which have never been surpassed for beauty of form and complete transfusion of the spirit of one literature into the language of another. On translation, however, he set but little store, asserting that he only undertook it when he "could do absolutely nothing else," and writing earnestly to dissuade Leigh Hunt from devoting time which might be better spent, to work of subordinate importance. (Letter from Florence, November 1819.) The following version of a Greek epigram on Plato's spirit will illustrate his own method of translation:—

Eagle! why soarest thou above that tomb?
To what sublime and star-y-paven home
Floatest thou?
I am the image of swift Plato's spirit,
Ascending heaven:—Athens does inherit
His corpse below.

Some time in the year 1820-21, he composed the "Defence of Poetry", stimulated to this undertaking by his friend Peacock's article on poetry, published in the Literary Miscellany. (See Letter to Ollier, January 20, 1820, Shelley Memorials, page 135.) This essay not only sets forth his theory of his own art, but it also contains some of his finest prose writing, of which the following passage, valuable alike for matter and style, may be cited as a specimen:—

"The functions of the poetical faculty are two-fold; by one it creates new materials of knowledge, and power, and pleasure; by the other it engenders in the mind a desire to reproduce and arrange them according to a certain rhythm and order which may be called the beautiful and the good. The cultivation of poetry is never more to be desired than at periods when, from an excess of the selfish and calculating principle, the accumulation of the materials of external life exceed the quantity of the power of assimilating them to the internal laws of human nature. The body has then become too unwieldy for that which animates it.

"Poetry is indeed something divine. It is at once the centre and circumference of knowledge; it is that which comprehends all science, and that to which all science must be referred. It is at the same time the root and blossom of all other systems of thought; it is that from which all spring, and that which adorns all; and that which, if blighted, denies the fruit and the seed, and withholds from the barren world the nourishment and the succession of the scions of the tree of life. It is the perfect and consummate surface and bloom of all things; it is as the odour and the colour of the rose to the texture of the elements which compose it, as the form and splendour of unfaded beauty to the secrets of anatomy and corruption. What were virtue, love, patriotism, friendship—what were the scenery of this beautiful universe which we inhabit— what were our consolations on this side of the grave—and what were our aspirations beyond it, if poetry did not ascend to bring light and fire from those eternal regions where the owl-winged faculty of calculation dare not ever soar? Poetry is not like reasoning, a power to be exerted according to the determination of the will. A man cannot say, "I will compose poetry." The greatest poet even cannot say it; for the mind in creation is as a fading coal, which some invisible influence, like an inconstant wind, awakens to transitory brightness; this power arises from within, like the colour of a flower which fades and changes as it is developed, and the conscious portions of our natures are unprophetic either of its approach or its departure. Could this influence be durable in its original purity and force, it is impossible to predict the greatness of the results; but when composition begins, inspiration is already on the decline, and the most glorious poetry that has ever been communicated to the world is probably a feeble shadow of the original conceptions of the poet. I appeal to the greatest poets of the present day, whether it is not an error to assert that the finest passages of poetry are produced by labour and study. The toil and the delay recommended by critics, can be justly interpreted to mean no more than a careful observation of the inspired moments, and an artificial connexion of the spaces between their suggestions by the intermixture of conventional expressions; a necessity only imposed by the limitedness of the poetical faculty itself; for Milton conceived the "Paradise Lost" as a whole before he executed it in portions. We have his own authority also for the muse having "dictated" to him the "unpremeditated song." And let this be an answer to those who would allege the fifty-six various readings of the first line of the "Orlando Furioso." Compositions so produced are to poetry what mosaic is to painting. This instinct and intuition of the poetical faculty is still more observable in the plastic and pictorial arts; a great statue or picture grows under the power of the artist as a child in the mother's womb; and the very mind which directs the hands in formation is incapable of accounting to itself for the origin, the gradations, or the media of the process.

"Poetry is the record of the best and happiest moments of the happiest and best minds. We are aware of evanescent visitations of thought and feeling sometimes associated with place or person, sometimes regarding our own mind alone, and always arising unforeseen and departing unbidden, but elevating and delightful beyond all expression: so that even in the desire and the regret they leave, there cannot but be pleasure, participating as it does in the nature of its object. It is as it were the interpenetration of a diviner nature through our own; but its footsteps are like those of a wind over the sea, which the coming calm erases, and whose traces remain only, as on the wrinkled sand which paves it. These and corresponding conditions of being are experienced principally by those of the most delicate sensibility and the most enlarged imagination; and the state of mind produced by them is at war with every base desire. The enthusiasm of virtue, love, patriotism, and friendship, is essentially linked with such emotions; and whilst they last, self appears as what it is, an atom to a universe. Poets are not only subject to these experiences as spirits of the most refined organization, but they can colour all that they combine with the evanescent hues of this ethereal world; a word, a trait in the representation of a scene or a passion, will touch the enchanted chord, and reanimate, in those who have ever experienced these emotions, the sleeping, the cold, the buried image of the past. Poetry thus makes immortal all that is best and most beautiful in the world; it arrests the vanishing apparitions which haunt the interlunations of life, and veiling them, or in language or in form, sends them forth among mankind, bearing sweet news of kindred joy to those with whom their sisters abide— abide, because there is no portal of expression from the caverns of the spirit which they inhabit into the universe of things. Poetry redeems from decay the visitations of the divinity in man."

In the midst of these aesthetic studies, and while producing his own greatest works, Shelley was not satisfied that his genius ought to be devoted to poetry. "I consider poetry," he wrote to Peacock, January 26th, 1819, "very subordinate to moral and political science, and if I were well, certainly I would aspire to the latter; for I can conceive a great work, embodying the discoveries of all ages, and harmonizing the contending creeds by which mankind have been ruled. Far from me is such an attempt, and I shall be content, by exercising my fancy, to amuse myself, and perhaps some others, and cast what weight I can into the scale of that balance which the Giant of Arthegall holds." Whether he was right in the conviction that his genius was no less fitted for metaphysical speculation or for political science than for poetry, is a question that admits of much debate. (See Mrs. Shelley's note on the Revolt of Islam, and the whole Preface to the Prose Works.) We have nothing but fragments whereby to form a definite opinion—the unfinished "Defence of Poetry", the unfinished "Essay on a Future State", the unfinished "Essay on Christianity", the unfinished "Essay on the Punishment of Death", and the scattered "Speculations on Metaphysics". None of these compositions justify the belief so confidently expressed by Mrs. Shelley in her Preface to the prose works, that "had not Shelley deserted metaphysics for poetry in his youth, and had he not been lost to us early, so that all his vaster projects were wrecked with him in the waves, he would have presented the world with a complete theory of mind; a theory to which Berkeley, Coleridge, and Kant would have contributed; but more simple, and unimpugnable, and entire than the systems of these writers." Their incompleteness rather tends to confirm what she proceeds to state, that the strain of philosophical composition was too great for his susceptible nerves; while her further observation that "thought kindled imagination and awoke sensation, and rendered him dizzy from too great keenness of emotion," seems to indicate that his nature was primarily that of a poet deeply tinctured with philosophical speculation, rather than that of a metaphysician warmed at intervals to an imaginative fervour. Another of her remarks confirms us in this opinion. "He considered these philosophical views of mind and nature to be instinct with the intensest spirit of poetry." (Note on Prometheus.) This is the position of the poet rather than the analyst; and on the whole, we are probably justified in concluding with Mrs. Shelley, that he followed a true instinct when he dedicated himself to poetry, and trained his powers in that direction. (Note on Revolt of Islam.) To dogmatize upon the topic would be worse than foolish. There was something incalculable, incommensurable, and daemonic in Shelley's genius; and what he might have achieved, had his life been spared and had his health progressively improved, it is of course impossible to say.

In the spring of 1819 the Shelleys settled in Rome, where the poet proceeded with the composition of "Prometheus Unbound". He used to write among the ruins of the Baths of Caracalla, not then, as now, despoiled of all their natural beauty, but waving with the Paradise of flowers and shrubs described in his incomparable letter of March the 23rd to Peacock. Rome, however, was not destined to retain them long. On the 7th of June they lost their son William after a short illness. Shelley loved this child intensely, and sat by his bedside for sixty hours without taking rest. He was now practically childless; and his grief found expression in many of his poems, especially in the fragment headed "Roma, Roma, Roma! non e piu com' era prima." William was buried in the Protestant cemetery, of which Shelley had written a description to Peacock in the previous December. "The English burying-place is a green slope near the walls, under the pyramidal tomb of Cestius, and is, I think, the most beautiful and solemn cemetery I ever beheld. To see the sun shining on its bright grass, fresh, when we first visited it, with the autumnal dews, and hear the whispering of the wind among the leaves of the trees which have overgrown the tomb of Cestius, and the soil which is stirring in the sun-warm earth, and to mark the tombs, mostly of women and young people who were buried there, one might, if one were to die, desire the sleep they seem to sleep. Such is the human mind, and so it peoples with its wishes vacancy and oblivion."

Escaping from the scene of so much sorrow, they established themselves at the Villa Valsovano, near Leghorn. Here Shelley began and finished "The Cenci" at the instance of his wife, who rightly thought that he undervalued his own powers as a dramatic poet. The supposed portrait of Beatrice in the Barberini Palace had powerfully affected his imagination, and he fancied that her story would form the fitting subject for a tragedy. It is fortunate for English literature that the real facts of that domestic drama, as recently published by Signor Bertolotti, were then involved in a tissue of romance and legend. During this summer he saw a great deal of the Gisborne family. Mrs. Gisborne's son by a previous marriage, Henry Reveley, was an engineer, and Shelley conceived a project of helping him build a steamer which should ply between Leghorn and Marseilles. He was to supply the funds, and the pecuniary profit was to be shared by the Gisborne family. The scheme eventually fell through, though Shelley spent a good deal of money upon it; and its only importance is the additional light it throws upon his public and private benevolence. From Leghorn the Shelleys removed in the autumn to Florence, where, on the 12th of November, the present Sir Percy Florence Shelley was born. Here Shelley wrote the last act of "Prometheus Unbound", which, though the finest portion of that unique drama, seems to have been an afterthought. In the Cascine outside Florence he also composed the "Ode to the West Wind", the most symmetrically perfect as well as the most impassioned of his minor lyrics. He spent much time in the galleries, made notes upon the principal antique statues, and formed a plan of systematic art-study. The climate, however, disagreed with him, and in the month of January, 1820, they took up their abode at Pisa.

1819 was the most important year in Shelley's life, so far as literary production is concerned. Besides "The Cenci" and "Prometheus Unbound", of which it yet remains to speak, this year saw the production of several political and satirical poems—the "Masque of Anarchy", suggested by the news of the Peterloo massacre, being by far the most important. Shelley attempted the composition of short popular songs which should stir the English people to a sense of what he felt to be their degradation. But he lacked the directness which alone could make such verses forcible, and the passionate apostrophe to the Men of England in his "Masque of Anarchy" marks the highest point of his achievement in this style:—

> Men of England, Heirs of Glory,
> Heroes of unwritten story,
> Nurslings of one mighty mother,
> Hopes of her, and one another!
>
> Rise, like lions after slumber,
> In unvanquishable number,
> Shake your chains to earth like dew,
> Which in sleep had fall'n on you.
> Ye are many, they are few.

"Peter Bell the Third", written in this year, and "Swellfoot the Tyrant", composed in the following autumn, are remarkable as showing with what keen interest Shelley watched public affairs in England from his exile home; but, for my own part, I cannot agree with those critics who esteem their humour at a high rate. The political poems may profitably be compared with his contemporary correspondence; with the letters, for instance, to Leigh Hunt, November 23rd, 1819; and to Mr. John Gisborne, April 10th, 1822; and with an undated fragment published by Mr. Garnett in the "Relics of Shelley", page 84. No student of English political history before the Reform Bill can regard his apprehensions of a great catastrophe as ill-founded. His insight into the real danger to the nation was as penetrating as his suggestion of a remedy was moderate. Those who are accustomed to think of the poet as a visionary enthusiast, will rub their eyes when they read the sober lines in which he warns his friend to be cautious about the security offered by the English Funds. Another letter, dated Lerici, June 29, 1822, illustrates the same practical temper of mind, the same logical application of political principles to questions of public economy.

That "Prometheus Unbound" and "The Cenci" should have been composed in one and the same year must be reckoned among the greatest wonders of literature, not only because of their sublime greatness, but also because of their essential difference. Aeschylus, it is well known, had written a sequel to his "Prometheus Bound", in which he showed the final reconciliation between Zeus, the oppressor, and Prometheus, the champion, of humanity. What that reconciliation was, we do not know, because the play is lost, and the fragments are too brief for supporting any probable hypothesis. But Shelley repudiated the notion of compromise. He could not conceive of the Titan "unsaying his high language, and quailing before his successful and perfidious adversary." He therefore, approached the theme of liberation from a wholly different point of view. Prometheus in his drama is the human vindicator of love, justice, and liberty, as opposed to Jove, the tyrannical oppressor, and creator of all evil by his selfish rule. Prometheus is the mind of man idealized, the spirit of our race, as Shelley thought it made to be. Jove is the incarnation of all that thwarts its free development. Thus counterposed, the two chief actors represent the fundamental antitheses of good and evil, liberty and despotism, love and hate. They give the form of personality to Shelley's Ormuzd-Ahriman dualism already expressed in the first canto of "Laon and Cythna"; but, instead of being represented on the theatre of human life, the strife is now removed into the reign of abstractions, vivified by mythopoetry. Prometheus resists Jove to the uttermost, endures all torments, physical and moral, that the tyrant plagues him with, secure in his own strength, and calmly expectant of an hour which shall hurl Jove from heaven, and leave the spirit of good triumphant. That hour arrives; Jove disappears; the burdens of the world and men are suddenly removed; a new age of peace and freedom and illimitable energy begins; the whole universe partakes in the emancipation; the spirit of the earth no longer groans in pain, but sings alternate love-songs with his sister orb, the moon; Prometheus is re-united in indissoluble bonds to his old love, Asia. Asia, withdrawn from sight during the first act, but spoken of as waiting in her exile for the fated hour, is the true mate of the human spirit. She is the fairest daughter of Earth and Ocean. Like Aphrodite, she rises in the Aegean near the land called by her name; and in the time of tribulation she dwells in a far Indian vale. She is the Idea of Beauty incarnate, the shadow of the Light of Life which sustains the world and enkindles it with love, the reality of Alastor's vision, the breathing image of the awful loveliness apostrophized in the "Hymn to Intellectual Beauty," the reflex of the splendour of which Adonais was a part. At the moment of her triumph she grows so beautiful that Ione her sister cannot see her, only feels her influence. The essential thought of Shelley's creed was that the universe is penetrated, vitalized, made real by a spirit, which he sometimes called the spirit of Nature, but which is always conceived as more than Life, as that which gives its actuality to Life, and lastly as Love and Beauty. To adore this spirit, to clasp it with affection, and to blend with it, is, he thought the true object of man. Therefore the final union of Prometheus with Asia is the consummation of human destinies. Love was the only law Shelley recognized. Unterrified by the grim realities of pain and crime revealed in nature and society, he held fast to the belief that, if we could but pierce to the core of things, if we could but be what we might be, the world and man would both attain to their perfection in eternal love. What resolution through some transcendental harmony was expected by Shelley for the palpable discords in the structure of the universe, we hardly know. He did not give his philosophy systematic form: and his new science of love remains a luminous poetic vision—nowhere more brilliantly set forth than in the "sevenfold hallelujahs and harping symphonies" of this, the final triumph of his lyrical poetry.

In "Prometheus", Shelley conceived a colossal work of art, and sketched out the main figures on a scale of surpassing magnificence. While painting in these figures, he seems to reduce their proportions too much to the level of earthly life. He quits his god-creating, heaven-compelling throne of mythopoeic inspiration, and descends to a love-story of Asia and Prometheus. In other words, he does not sustain the visionary and primeval dignity of these incarnated abstractions; nor, on the other hand, has he so elaborated their characters in detail as to give them the substantiality of persons. There is therefore something vague and hollow in both figures. Yet in the subordinate passages of the poem, the true mythopoeic faculty—the faculty of finding concrete forms for thought, and of investing emotion with personality—shines forth with extraordinary force and clearness. We feel ourselves in the grasp of a primitive myth-maker while we read the description of Oceanus, and the raptures of the Earth and Moon.

A genuine liking for "Prometheus Unbound" may be reckoned the touch-stone of a man's capacity for understanding lyric poetry. The world in which the action is supposed to move, rings with spirit voices; and what these spirits sing, is melody more purged of mortal dross than any other poet's ear has caught, while listening to his own heart's song, or to the rhythms of the world. There are hymns in "Prometheus", which seem to realize the miracle of making words, detached from meaning, the substance of a new ethereal music; and yet, although their verbal harmony is such, they are never devoid of definite significance for those who understand. Shelley scorned the aesthetics of a school which finds "sense swooning into nonsense" admirable. And if a critic is so dull as to ask what "Life of Life! thy lips enkindle" means, or to whom it is addressed, none can help him any more than one can help a man whose sense of hearing is too gross for the tenuity of a bat's cry. A voice in the air thus sings the hymn of Asia at the moment of her apotheosis:—

> Life of Life! thy lips enkindle
> With their love the breath between them;
> And thy smiles before they dwindle
> Make the cold air fire; then screen them
> In those looks where whoso gazes
> Faints, entangled in their mazes.
>
> Child of Light! thy limbs are burning
> Through the vest which seems to hide them,
> As the radiant lines of morning
> Through the clouds, ere they divide them;
> And this atmosphere divinest
> Shrouds thee whereso'er thou shinest.
>
> Fair are others; none beholds thee.
> But thy voice sounds low and tender,
> Like the fairest, for it folds thee
> From the sight, that liquid splendour,
> And all feel, yet see thee never,
> As I feel now, lost for ever!

Lamp of Earth! where'er thou movest
Its dim shapes are clad with brightness,
And the souls of whom thou lovest
Walk upon the winds with lightness,
Till they fail, as I am failing,
Dizzy, lost, yet unbewailing!

It has been said that Shelley, as a landscape painter, is decidedly Turneresque; and there is much in "Prometheus Unbound" to justify this opinion. The scale of colour is light and aerial, and the darker shadows are omitted. An excess of luminousness seems to be continually radiated from the objects at which he looks; and in this radiation of many-coloured lights, the outline itself is apt to be a little misty. Shelley, moreover, pierced through things to their spiritual essence. The actual world was less for him than that which lies within it and beyond it. "I seek," he says himself, "in what I see, the manifestation of something beyond the present and tangible object." For him, as for the poet described by one of the spirit voices in "Prometheus", the bees in the ivy-bloom are scarcely heeded; they become in his mind,—

Forms more real than living man,
Nurslings of immortality.

And yet who could have brought the bees, the lake, the sun, the bloom, more perfectly before us than that picture does? (Forman, volume 2 page 181.) What vignette is more exquisitely coloured and finished than the little study of a pair of halcyons in the third act? (Forman, volume 2 page 231.) Blake is perhaps the only artist who could have illustrated this drama. He might have shadowed forth the choirs of spirits, the trailing voices and their thrilling songs, phantasmal Demorgorgon, and the charioted Hour. Prometheus, too, with his "flowing limbs," has just Blake's fault of impersonation—the touch of unreality in that painter's Adam.

Passing to "The Cenci", we change at once the moral and artistic atmosphere. The lyrical element, except for one most lovely dirge, is absent. Imagery and description are alike sternly excluded. Instead of soaring to the empyrean, our feet are firmly planted on the earth. In exchange for radiant visions of future perfection, we are brought into the sphere of dreadful passions—all the agony, endurance, and half-maddened action, of which luckless human innocence is capable. To tell the legend of Beatrice Cenci here, is hardly needed. Her father, a monster of vice and cruelty, was bent upon breaking her spirit by imprisonment, torture, and nameless outrage. At last her patience ended; and finding no redress in human justice, no champion of her helplessness in living man, she wrought his death. For this she died upon the scaffold, together with her step-mother and her brothers, who had aided in the execution of the murder. The interest of "The Cenci", and it is overwhelmingly great, centres in Beatrice and her father; from these two chief actors in the drama, all the other characters fall away into greater or less degrees of unsubstantiality. Perhaps Shelley intended this—as the maker of a bas-relief contrives two or three planes of figures for the presentation of his ruling group. Yet there appears to my mind a defect of accomplishment, rather than a deliberate intention, in the delineation of Orsino. He seems meant to be the wily, crafty, Machiavellian reptile, whose calculating wickedness should form a contrast to the daemonic, reckless, almost maniacal fiendishness of old Francesco Cenci. But this conception of him wavers; his love for Beatrice is too delicately tinted, and he is suffered to break down with an infirmity of conscience alien to such a nature. On the other hand the uneasy vacillations of Giacomo, and the irresolution, born of feminine weakness and want of fibre, in Lucrezia, serve to throw the firm will of Beatrice into prominent relief; while her innocence, sustained through extraordinary suffering in circumstances of exceptional horror—the innocence of a noble nature thrust by no act of its own but by its wrongs beyond the pale of ordinary womankind—is contrasted with the merely childish guiltlessness of Bernardo. Beatrice rises to her full height in the fifth act, dilates and grows with the approach of danger, and fills the whole scene with her spirit on the point of death. Her sublime confidence in the justice and essential rightness of her action, the glance of self-assured purity with which she annihilates the cut-throat brought to testify against her, her song in prison, and her tender solicitude for the frailer Lucrezia, are used with wonderful dramatic skill for the fulfilment of a feminine ideal at once delicate and powerful. Once and once only does she yield to ordinary weakness; it is when the thought crosses her mind that she may meet her father in the other world, as once he came to her on earth.

Shelley dedicated "The Cenci" to Leigh Hunt, saying that he had striven in this tragedy to cast aside the subjective manner of his earlier work, and to produce something at once more popular and more concrete, more sober in style, and with a firmer grasp on the realities of life. He was very desirous of getting it acted, and wrote to Peacock requesting him to offer it at Covent Garden. Miss O'Neil, he thought, would play the part of Beatrice admirably. The manager, however, did not take this view; averring that the subject rendered it incapable of being even submitted to an actress like Miss O'Neil. Shelley's self-criticism is always so valuable, that it may be well here to collect what he said about the two great dramas of 1819. Concerning "The Cenci" he wrote to Peacock:—"It is written without any of the peculiar feelings and opinions which characterize my other compositions; I having attended simply to the impartial development of such characters as it is probable the persons represented really were, together with the greatest degree of popular effect to be produced by such a development." "'Cenci' is written for the multitude, and ought to sell well." "I believe it singularly fitted for the stage." "'The Cenci' is a work of art; it is not coloured by my feelings, nor obscured by my metaphysics. I don't think much of it. It gave me less trouble than anything I have written of the same length." "Prometheus", on the other hand, he tells Ollier, "is my favourite poem; I charge you, therefore, specially to pet him and feed him with fine ink and good paper"—which was duly done. Again:—"For 'Prometheus', I expect and desire no great sale; Prometheus was never intended for more than five or six persons; it is in my judgment of a higher character than anything I have yet attempted, and is perhaps less an imitation of anything that has gone before it; it is original, and cost me severe mental labour." Shelley was right in judging that "The Cenci" would be comparatively popular; this was proved by the fact that it went through two editions in his lifetime. The value he set upon "Prometheus" as the higher work, will hardly be disputed. Unique in the history of literature, and displaying the specific qualities of its author at their height, the world could less easily afford to lose this drama than "The Cenci", even though that be the greatest tragedy composed in English since the death of Shakespeare. For reasons which will be appreciated by lovers of dramatic poetry, I refrain from detaching portions of these two plays. Those who desire to make themselves acquainted with the author's genius, must devote long and patient study to the originals in their entirety.

"Prometheus Unbound", like the majority of Shelley's works, fell still-born from the press. It furnished punsters with a joke, however, which went the round of several papers; this poem, they cried, is well named, for who would bind it? Of criticism that deserves the name, Shelley got absolutely nothing in his lifetime. The stupid but venomous reviews which gave him occasional pain, but which he mostly laughed at, need not now be mentioned. It is not much to any purpose to abuse the authors of mere rubbish. The real lesson to be learned from such of them as may possibly have been sincere, as well as from the failure of his contemporaries to appreciate his genius—the sneers of Moore, the stupidity of Campbell, the ignorance of Wordsworth, the priggishness of Southey, or the condescending tone of Keats—is that nothing is more difficult than for lesser men or equals to pay just homage to the greatest in their lifetime. Those who may be interested in studying Shelley's attitude toward his critics, should read a letter addressed to Ollier from Florence, October 15, 1819, soon after he had seen the vile attack upon him in the "Quarterly", comparing this with the fragments of an expostulatory letter to the Editor, and the preface to "Adonais". (Shelley Memorials, page 121. Garnett's Relics of Shelley, pages 49, 190. Collected Letters, page 147, in Moxon's Edition of Works in one volume 1840.) It is clear that, though he bore scurrilous abuse with patience, he was prepared if needful to give blow for blow. On the 11th of June, 1821, he wrote to Ollier:—"As yet I have laughed; but woe to those scoundrels if they should once make me lose my temper!" The stanzas on the "Quarterly" in "Adonais", and the invective against Lord Eldon, show what Shelley could have done if he had chosen to castigate the curs. Meanwhile the critics achieved what they intended. Shelley, as Trelawny emphatically tells us, was universally shunned, coldly treated by Byron's friends at Pisa, and regarded as a monster by such of the English in Italy as had not made his personal acquaintance. On one occasion he is even said to have been knocked down in a post-office by some big bully, who escaped before he could obtain his name and address; but this is one of the stories rendered doubtful by the lack of precise details.

CHAPTER 6

RESIDENCE AT PISA

ON the 26th of January, 1820, the Shelley's established themselves at Pisa. From this date forward to the 7th of July, 1822, Shelley's life divides itself into two periods of unequal length; the first spent at Pisa, the baths of San Giuliano, and Leghorn; the second at Lerici, on the Bay of Spezia. Without entering into minute particulars of dates or recording minor changes of residence, it is possible to treat of the first and longer period in general. The house he inhabited at Pisa was on the south side of the Arno. After a few months he became the neighbour of Lord Byron, who engaged the Palazzo Lanfranchi it order to be near him; and here many English and Italian friends gathered round them. Among these must be mentioned in the first place Captain Medwin, whose recollections of the Pisan residence are of considerable value, and next Captain Trelawny, who has left a record of Shelley's last days only equalled in vividness by Hogg's account of the Oxford period, and marked by signs of more unmistakable accuracy. Not less important members of this private circle were Mr. and Mrs. Edward Elleker Williams, with whom Shelley and his wife lived on terms of the closest friendship. Among Italians, the physician Vacca, the improvisatore Sgricci, and Rosini, the author of "La Monaca di Monza", have to be recorded. It will be seen from this enumeration that Shelley was no longer solitary; and indeed it would appear that now, upon the eve of his accidental death, he had begun to enjoy an immunity from many of his previous sufferings. Life expanded before him: his letters show that he was concentrating his powers and preparing for a fresh flight; and the months, though ever productive of poetic masterpieces, promised a still more magnificent birth in the future.

In the summer and autumn of 1820, Shelley produced some of his most genial poems: the "Letter to Maria Gisborne", which might be mentioned as a pendent to "Julian and Maddalo" for its treatment of familiar things; the "Ode to a Skylark", that most popular of all his lyrics; the "Witch of Atlas", unrivalled as an Ariel-flight of fairy fancy; and the "Ode to Naples", which, together with the "Ode to Liberty", added a new lyric form to English literature. In the winter he wrote the "Sensitive Plant", prompted thereto, we are told, by the flowers which crowded Mrs. Shelley's drawing room, and exhaled their sweetness to the temperate Italian sunlight. Whether we consider the number of these poems or their diverse character, ranging from verse separated by an exquisitely subtle line from simple prose to the most impassioned eloquence and the most ethereal imagination, we shall be equally astonished. Every chord of the poet's lyre is touched, from the deep bass string that echoes the diurnal speech of such a man as Shelley was, to the fine vibrations of a treble merging its rarity of tone in accents super-sensible to ordinary ears. One passage from the "Letter to Maria Gisborne" may here be quoted, not for its poetry, but for the light it casts upon the circle of his English friends.

You are now
In London, that great sea, whose ebb and flow
At once is deaf and loud, and on the shore
Vomits its wrecks, and still howls on for more.
Yet in its depth what treasures! You will see
That which was Godwin,—greater none than he
Though fallen—and fallen on evil times—to stand
Among the spirits of our age and land,
Before the dread tribunal of "To come"
The foremost, while Rebuke cowers pale and dumb.
You will see Coleridge—he who sits obscure
In the exceeding lustre and the pure
Intense irradiation of a mind,
Which, with its own internal lightning blind,
Flags wearily through darkness and despair—
A cloud-encircled meteor of the air,
A hooded eagle among blinking owls.
You will see Hunt; one of those happy souls
Which are the salt of the earth, and without whom
This world would smell like what it is—a tomb;
Who is, what others seem. His room no doubt
Is still adorned by many a cast from Shout,
With graceful flowers tastefully placed about,
And coronals of bay from ribbons hung,
And brighter wreaths in neat disorder flung;
The gifts of the most learn'd among some dozens
Of female friends, sisters-in-law, and cousins.
And there is he with his eternal puns,
Which beat the dullest brain for smiles, like duns
Thundering for money at a poet's door;
Alas! it is no use to say, "I'm poor!"—
Or oft in graver mood, when he will look
Things wiser than were ever read in book,
Except in Shakespere's wisest tenderness.
You will see Hogg; and I cannot express
His virtues, though I know that they are great,
Because he locks, then barricades the gate
Within which they inhabit. Of his wit
And wisdom, you'll cry out when you are bit.
He is a pearl within an oyster-shell,
One of the richest of the deep. And there
Is English Peacock, with his mountain fair,—
Turn'd into a Flamingo, that shy bird
That gleams in the Indian air. Have you not heard
When a man marries, dies, or turns Hindoo,

His best friends hear no more of him. But you
Will see him, and will like him too, I hope,
With the milk-white Snowdownian antelope
Match'd with this camelopard. His fine wit
Makes such a wound, the knife is lost in it;
A strain too learned for a shallow age,
Too wise for selfish bigots; let his page
Which charms the chosen spirits of the time,
Fold itself up for the serener clime
Of years to come, and find its recompense
In that just expectation. Wit and sense,
Virtue and human knowledge, all that might
Make this dull world a business of delight,
Are all combined in Horace Smith. And these,
With some exceptions, which I need not tease
Your patience by descanting on, are all
You and I know in London.

Captain Medwin, who came late in the autumn of 1820, at his cousin's invitation, to stay with the Shelleys, has recorded many interesting details of their Pisan life, as well as valuable notes of Shelley's conversation. "It was nearly seven years since we had parted, but I should have immediately recognized him in a crowd. His figure was emaciated, and somewhat bent, owing to near-sightedness, and his being forced to lean over his books, with his eyes almost touching them; his hair, still profuse, and curling naturally, was partially interspersed with grey; but his appearance was youthful. There was also a freshness and purity in his complexion that he never lost." Not long after his arrival, Medwin suffered from a severe and tedious illness. "Shelley tended me like a brother. He applied my leeches, administered my medicines, and during six weeks that I was confined to my room, was assiduous and unintermitting in his affectionate care of me." The poet's solitude and melancholy at this time impressed his cousin very painfully. Though he was producing a long series of imperishable poems, he did not take much interest in his work. "I am disgusted with writing," he once said, "and were it not for an irresistible impulse, that predominates my better reason, should discontinue so doing." The brutal treatment he had lately received from the "Quarterly Review", the calumnies which pursued him, and the coldness of all but a very few friends, checked his enthusiasm for composition. Of this there are abundant proof in his correspondence. In a letter to Leigh Hunt, dated January 25, 1822, he says: "My faculties are shaken to atoms and torpid. I can write nothing; and if "Adonais" had no success, and excited no interest, what incentive can I have to write?" Again: "I write little now. It is impossible to compose except under the strong excitement of an assurance of finding sympathy in what you write." Lord Byron's company proved now, as before, a check rather than an incentive to production: "I do not write; I have lived too long near Lord Byron, and the sun has extinguished the glow-worm; for I cannot hope, with St. John, that THE LIGHT CAME INTO THE WORLD AND THE WORLD KNEW IT NOT." "I despair of rivalling Lord Byron, as well I may, and there is no other with whom it is worth contending." To Ollier, in 1820, he wrote: "I doubt whether I shall write more. I could be content either with the hell or the paradise of poetry; but the torments of its purgatory vex me, without exciting my powers sufficiently to put an end to the vexation." It was not that his spirit was cowed by the Reviews, or that he mistook the sort of audience he had to address. He more than once acknowledged that, while Byron wrote for the many, his poems were intended for the understanding few. Yet the sunetoi, as he called them, gave him but scanty encouragement. The cold phrases of kindly Horace Smith show that he had not comprehended "Prometheus Unbound"; and Shelley whimsically complains that even intelligent and sympathetic critics confounded the ideal passion described in "Epipsychidion" with the love affairs of "a servant-girl and her sweetheart." This almost incomprehensible obtuseness on the part of men who ought to have known better, combined with the coarse abuse of vulgar scribblers, was enough to make a man so sincerely modest as Shelley doubt his powers, or shrink from the severe labour of developing them. (See Medwin, volume 2 page 172, for Shelley's comment on the difficulty of the poet's art.) "The decision of the cause," he wrote to Mr. Gisborne, "whether or no I am a poet, is removed from the present time to the hour when our posterity shall assemble; but the court is a very severe one, and I fear that the verdict will be, guilty—death." Deep down in his own heart he had, however, less doubt: "This I know," he said to Medwin, "that whether in prosing or in versing, there is something in my writings that shall live for ever." And again, he writes to Hunt: "I am full of thoughts and plans, and should do something, if the feeble and irritable frame which encloses it was willing to obey the spirit. I fancy that then I should do great things." It seems almost certain that the incompleteness of many longer works designed in the Italian period, the abandonment of the tragedy on Tasso's story, the unfinished state of "Charles I", and the failure to execute the cherished plan of a drama suggested by the Book of Job, were due to the depressing effects of ill-health and external discouragement. Poetry with Shelley was no light matter. He composed under the pressure of intense excitement, and he elaborated his first draughts with minute care and severe self-criticism.

These words must not be taken as implying that he followed the Virgilian precedent of polishing and reducing the volume of his verses by an anxious exercise of calm reflection, or that he observed the Horatian maxim of deferring their publication till the ninth year. The contrary was notoriously the case with him. Yet it is none the less proved by the state of his manuscripts that his compositions, even as we now possess them, were no mere improvisations. The passage already quoted from his "Defence of Poetry" shows the high ideal he had conceived of the poet's duty toward his art; and it may be confidently asserted that his whole literary career was one long struggle to emerge from the incoherence of his earlier efforts, into the clearness of expression and precision of form that are the index of mastery over style. At the same time it was inconsistent with his most firmly rooted aesthetic principles to attempt composition except under an impulse approaching to inspiration. To imperil his life by the fiery taxing of all his faculties, moral, intellectual, and physical, and to undergo the discipline exacted by his own fastidious taste, with no other object in view than the frigid compliments of a few friends, was more than even Shelley's enthusiasm could endure. He, therefore, at this period required the powerful stimulus of some highly exciting cause from without to determine his activity.

Such external stimulus came to Shelley from three quarters early in the year 1821. Among his Italian acquaintances at Pisa was a clever but disreputable Professor, of whom Medwin draws a very piquant portrait. This man one day related the sad story of a beautiful and noble lady, the Contessina Emilia Viviani, who had been confined by her father in a dismal convent of the suburbs, to await her marriage with a distasteful husband. Shelley, fired as ever by a tale of tyranny, was eager to visit the fair captive. The Professor accompanied him and Medwin to the convent-parlour, where they found her more lovely than even the most glowing descriptions had led them to expect. Nor was she only beautiful. Shelley soon discovered that she had "cultivated her mind beyond what I have ever met in Italian women;" and a rhapsody composed by her upon the subject of Uranian Love—Il Vero Amore—justifies the belief that she possessed an intellect of more than ordinary elevation. He took Mrs. Shelley to see her, and both did all they could to make her convent-prison less irksome, by frequent visits, by letters, and by presents of flowers and books. It was not long before Shelley's sympathy for this unfortunate lady took the form of love, which, however spiritual and Platonic, was not the less passionate. The result was the composition of "Epipsychidion," the most unintelligible of all his poems to those who have not assimilated the spirit of Plato's "Symposium" and Dante's "Vita Nuova". In it he apostrophizes Emilia Viviani as the incarnation of ideal beauty, the universal loveliness made visible in mortal flesh:—

> Seraph of Heaven! too gentle to be human,
> Veiling beneath that radiant form of woman
> All that is insupportable in thee
> Of light, and love, and immortality!

He tells her that he loves her, and describes the troubles and deceptions of his earlier manhood, under allegories veiled in delicate obscurity. The Pandemic and the Uranian Aphrodite have striven for his soul; for though in youth he dedicated himself to the service of ideal beauty, and seemed to find it under many earthly shapes, yet has he ever been deluded. At last Emily appears, and in her he recognizes the truth of the vision veiled from him so many years. She and Mary shall henceforth, like sun and moon, rule the world of love within him. Then he calls on her to fly. They three will escape and live together, far away from men, in an Aegean island. The description of this visionary isle, and of the life to be led there by the fugitives from a dull and undiscerning world, is the most beautiful that has been written this century in the rhymed heroic metre.

It is an isle under Ionian skies,
Beautiful as a wreck of Paradise;
And, for the harbours are not safe and good,
This land would have remained a solitude
But for some pastoral people native there,
Who from the Elysian, clear, and golden air
Draw the last spirit of the age of gold,
Simple and spirited, innocent and bold.
The blue Aegean girds this chosen home,
With ever-changing sound and light and foam
Kissing the sifted sands and caverns hoar;
And all the winds wandering along the shore,
Undulate with the undulating tide.
There are thick woods where sylvan forms abide;
And many a fountain, rivulet, and pond,
As clear as elemental diamond,
Or serene morning air. And far beyond,
The mossy tracks made by the goats and deer,
(Which the rough shepherd treads but once a year,)
Pierce into glades, caverns, and bowers, and halls
Built round with ivy, which the waterfalls
Illumining, with sound that never fails
Accompany the noonday nightingales;
And all the place is peopled with sweet airs.
The light clear element which the isle wears
Is heavy with the scent of lemon-flowers,
Which floats like mist laden with unseen showers,
And falls upon the eyelids like faint sleep;
And from the moss violets and jonquils peep,
And dart the arrowy odour through the brain,
Till you might faint with that delicious pain.
And every motion, odour, beam, and tone,
With that deep music is in unison:
Which is a soul within a soul—they seem
Like echoes of an antenatal dream.
It is an isle 'twixt heaven, air, earth, and sea,
Cradled, and hung in clear tranquillity;
Bright as that wandering Eden, Lucifer,
Washed by the soft blue oceans of young air.
It is a favoured place. Famine or Blight,
Pestilence, War, and Earthquake, never light
Upon its mountain-peaks; blind vultures, they

Sail onward far upon their fatal way.
The winged storms, chanting their thunder-psalm
To other lands, leave azure chasms of calm
Over this isle, or weep themselves in dew,
From which its fields and woods ever renew
Their green and golden immortality.
And from the sea there rise, and from the sky
There fall, clear exhalations, soft and bright,
Veil after veil, each hiding some delight,
Which sun or moon or zephyr draws aside,
Till the isle's beauty, like a naked bride
Glowing at once with love and loveliness,
Blushes and trembles at its own excess:
Yet, like a buried lamp, a soul no less
Burns in the heart of this delicious isle,
An atom of the Eternal, whose own smile
Unfolds itself, and may be felt not seen
O'er the grey rocks, blue waves, and forests green,
Filling their bare and void interstices.

Shelley did not publish "Epipsychidion" with his own name. He gave it to the world as a composition of a man who had "died at Florence, as he was preparing for a voyage to one of the Sporades," and he requested Ollier not to circulate it, except among a few intelligent readers. It may almost be said to have been never published, in such profound silence did it issue from the press. Very shortly after its appearance he described it to Leigh Hunt as "a portion of me already dead," and added this significant allusion to its subject matter:—"Some of us have in a prior existence been in love with Antigone, and that makes us find no full content in any mortal tie." In the letter of June 18, 1822, again he says:—"The 'Epipsychidion' I cannot look at; the person whom it celebrates was a cloud instead of a Juno; and poor Ixion starts from the Centaur that was the offspring of his own embrace. If you are curious, however, to hear what I am and have been, it will tell you something thereof. It is an idealized history of my life and feelings. I think one is always in love with something or other; the error, and I confess it is not easy for spirits cased in flesh and blood to avoid it, consists in seeking in a mortal image the likeness of what is, perhaps, eternal." This paragraph contains the essence of a just criticism. Brilliant as the poem is, we cannot read it with unwavering belief either in the author's sincerity at the time he wrote it, or in the permanence of the emotion it describes. The exordium has a fatal note of rhetorical exaggeration, not because the kind of passion is impossible, but because Shelley does not convince us that in this instance he had really been its subject. His own critique, following so close upon the publication of "Epipsychidion," confirms the impression made by it, and justifies the conclusion that he had utilized his feeling for Emilia to express a favourite doctrine in impassioned verse.

To students of Shelley's inner life "Epipsychidion" will always have high value, independently of its beauty of style, as containing his doctrine of love. It is the full expression of the esoteric principle presented to us in "Alastor", the "Hymn to Intellectual Beauty," and "Prince Athanase." But the words just quoted, which may be compared with Mrs. Shelley's note to "Prince Athanase," authorize our pointing out what he himself recognized as the defect of his theory. Instead of remaining true to the conception of Beauty expressed in the "Hymn," Shelley "sought through the world the One whom he may love." Thus, while his doctrine in "Epipsychidion" seems Platonic, it will not square with the "Symposium." Plato treats the love of a beautiful person as a mere initiation into divine mysteries, the first step in the ladder that ascends to heaven. When a man has formed a just conception of the universal beauty, he looks back with a smile upon those who find their soul's sphere in the love of some mere mortal object. Tested by this standard, Shelley's identification of Intellectual Beauty with so many daughters of earth, and his worshipping love of Emilia, is a spurious Platonism. Plato would have said that to seek the Idea of Beauty in Emilia Viviani was a retrogressive step. All that she could do, would be to quicken the soul's sense of beauty, to stir it from its lethargy, and to make it divine the eternal reality of beauty in the supersensual world of thought. This Shelley had already acknowledged in the "Hymn;" and this he emphasizes in these words:— "The error consists in seeking in a mortal image the likeness of what is, perhaps, eternal."

The fragments and cancelled passages published in Forman's edition do not throw much light upon "Epipsychidion." The longest, entitled "To his Genius" by its first editor, Mr. Garnett, reads like the induction to a poem conceived and written in a different key, and at a lower level of inspiration. It has, however, this extraordinary interest, that it deals with a love which is both love and friendship, above sex, spiritual, unintelligible to the world at large. Thus the fragment enables the student better to realize the kind of worship so passionately expressed in "Epipsychidion."

The news of Keats's death at Rome on the 27th of December, 1820, and the erroneous belief that it had been accelerated, if not caused, by a contemptible review of "Endymion" in the "Quarterly", stirred Shelley to the composition of "Adonais". He had it printed at Pisa, and sent copies to Ollier for circulation in London. This poem was a favourite with its author, who hoped not only that it might find acceptance with the public, but also that it would confer lustre upon the memory of a poet whom he sincerely admired. No criticisms upon Shelley's works are half so good as his own. It is, therefore, interesting to collect the passages in which he speaks of an elegy only equalled in our language by "Lycidas", and in the point of passionate eloquence even superior to Milton's youthful lament for his friend. "The 'Adonais', in spite of its mysticism," he writes to Ollier, "is the least imperfect of my compositions." "I confess I should be surprised if that poem were born to an immortality of oblivion." "It is a highly wrought PIECE OF ART, and perhaps better, in point of composition, than anything I have written." "It is absurd in any review to criticize 'Adonais', and still more to pretend that the verses are bad." "I know what to think of 'Adonais', but what to think of those who confound it with the many bad poems of the day, I know not." Again, alluding to the stanzas hurled against the infamous "Quarterly" reviewer, he says:—"I have dipped my pen in consuming fire for his destroyers; otherwise the style is calm and solemn."

With these estimates the reader of to-day will cordially agree. Although "Adonais" is not so utterly beyond the scope of other poets as "Prometheus" or "Epipsychidion," it presents Shelley's qualities in a form of even and sustained beauty, brought within the sphere of the dullest apprehensions. Shelley, we may notice, dwells upon the ART of the poem; and this perhaps, is what at first sight will strike the student most. He chose as a foundation for his work those laments of Bion for Adonis, and of Moschus for Bion, which are the most pathetic products of Greek idyllic poetry; and the transmutation of their material into the substance of highly spiritualized modern thought, reveals the potency of a Prospero's wand. It is a metamorphosis whereby the art of excellent but positive poets has been translated into the sphere of metaphysical imagination. Urania takes the place of Aphrodite; the thoughts and fancies and desires of the dead singer are substituted for Bion's cupids; and instead of mountain shepherds, the living bards of England are summoned to lament around the poet's bier. Yet it is only when Shelley frees himself from the influence of his models, that he soars aloft on mighty wing. This point, too, is the point of transition from death, sorrow, and the past to immortality, joy, and the rapture of the things that cannot pass away. The first and second portions of the poem are, at the same time, thoroughly concordant, and the passage from the one to the other is natural. Two quotations from "Adonais" will suffice to show the power and sweetness of its verse.

The first is a description of Shelley himself following Byron and Moore— the "Pilgrim of Eternity," and Ierne's "sweetest lyrist of her saddest wrong"—to the couch where Keats lies dead. There is both pathos and unconscious irony in his making these two poets the chief mourners, when we remember what Byron wrote about Keats in "Don Juan", and what Moore afterwards recorded of Shelley; and when we think, moreover, how far both Keats and Shelley have outsoared Moore, and disputed with Byron his supreme place in the heaven of poetry.

> Midst others of less note, came one frail Form,
> A phantom among men, companionless
> As the last cloud of an expiring storm,
> Whose thunder is its knell. He, as I guess,
> Had gazed on Nature's naked loveliness,
> Actaeon-like, and now he fled astray
> With feeble steps o'er the world's wilderness,
> And his own thoughts, along that rugged way,
> Pursued like raging hounds their father and their prey.

A pard-like Spirit beautiful and swift—
A love in desolation masked—a Power
Girt round with weakness; it can scarce uplift
The weight of the superincumbent hour;
Is it a dying lamp, a falling shower,
A breaking billow;—even whilst we speak
Is it not broken? On the withering flower
The killing sun smiles brightly: on a cheek
The life can burn in blood, even while the heart may break.

His head was bound with pansies over-blown,
And faded violets, white and pied and blue;
And a light spear topped with a cypress cone,
Round whose rude shaft dark ivy-tresses grew
Yet dripping with the forest's noon-day dew,
Vibrated, as the ever-beating heart
Shook the weak hand that grasped it. Of that crew
He came the last, neglected and apart;
A herd-abandoned deer, struck by the hunter's dart.

The second passage is the peroration of the poem. Nowhere has Shelley expressed his philosophy of man's relation to the universe with more sublimity and with a more imperial command of language than in these stanzas. If it were possible to identify that philosophy with any recognized system of thought, it might be called pantheism. But it is difficult to affix a name, stereotyped by the usage of the schools, to the aerial spiritualism of its ardent and impassioned poet's creed.

The movement of the long melodious sorrow-song has just been interrupted by three stanzas, in which Shelley lashes the reviewer of Keats. He now bursts forth afresh into the music of consolation:—

Peace, peace! he is not dead, he doth not sleep!
He hath awakened from the dream of life.
'Tis we who, lost in stormy visions, keep
With phantoms an unprofitable strife,
And in mad trance strike with our spirit's knife
Invulnerable nothings. WE decay
Like corpses in a charnel; fear and grief
Convulse us and consume us day by day,
And cold hopes swarm like worms within our living clay.

He has outsoared the shadow of our night;
Envy and calumny, and hate and pain,
And that unrest which men miscall delight,
Can touch him not and torture not again;

From the contagion of the world's slow stain
He is secure, and now can never mourn
A heart grown cold, a head grown grey in vain;
Nor, when the spirit's self has ceased to burn,
With sparkless ashes load an unlamented urn.

He lives, he wakes—'tis Death is dead, not he;
Mourn not for Adonais.—Thou young Dawn,
Turn all thy dew to splendour, for from thee
The spirit thou lamentest is not gone;
Ye caverns and ye forests, cease to moan!
Cease, ye faint flowers and fountains, and thou Air
Which like a mourning veil thy scarf hadst thrown
O'er the abandoned Earth, now leave it bare
Even to the joyous stars which smile on its despair!

He is made one with Nature: there is heard
His voice in all her music, from the moan
Of thunder, to the song of night's sweet bird;
He is a presence to be felt and known
In darkness and in light, from herb and stone,
Spreading itself where'er that Power may move
Which has withdrawn his being to its own;
Which wields the world with never wearied love,
Sustains it from beneath, and kindles it above.

He is a portion of the loveliness
Which once he made more lovely: he doth bear
His part, while the One Spirit's plastic stress
Sweeps through the dull dense world, compelling there
All new successions to the forms they wear;
Torturing th' unwilling dross that checks its flight
To its own likeness, as each mass may bear;
And bursting in its beauty and its might
From trees and beasts and men into the Heaven's light.

But the absorption of the human soul into primeval nature-forces, the blending of the principle of thought with the universal spirit of beauty, is not enough to satisfy man's yearning after immortality. Therefore in the next three stanzas the indestructibility of the personal self is presented to us, as the soul of Adonais passes into the company of the illustrious dead who, like him, were untimely slain:—

The splendours of the firmament of time
May be eclipsed, but are extinguished not:

Like stars to their appointed height they climb,
And death is a low mist which cannot blot
The brightness it may veil. When lofty thought
Lifts a young heart above its mortal lair,
And love and life contend in it, for what
Shall be its earthly doom, the dead live there,
And move like winds of light on dark and stormy air.

The inheritors of unfulfilled renown
Rose from their thrones, built beyond mortal thought,
Far in the Unapparent. Chatterton
Rose pale, his solemn agony had not
Yet faded from him; Sidney, as he fought
And as he fell, and as he lived and loved,
Sublimely mild, a Spirit without spot,
Arose; and Lucan, by his death approved:—
Oblivion as they rose shrank like a thing reproved.

And many more, whose names on Earth are dark,
But whose transmitted effluence cannot die
So long as fire outlives the parent spark,
Rose, robed in dazzling immortality.
"Thou art become as one of us," they cry;
"It was for thee yon kingless sphere has long
Swung blind in unascended majesty,
Silent alone amid an Heaven of song.
Assume thy winged throne, thou Vesper of our throng!"

From the more universal and philosophical aspects of his theme, the poet once more turns to the special subject that had stirred him. Adonais lies dead; and those who mourn him must seek his grave. He has escaped: to follow him is to die; and where should we learn to dote on death unterrified, if not in Rome? In this way the description of Keat's resting-place beneath the pyramid of Cestius, which was also destined to be Shelley's own, is introduced:—

Who mourns for Adonais? oh come forth,
Fond wretch! and show thyself and him aright.
Clasp with thy panting soul the pendulous Earth;
As from a centre, dart thy spirit's light
Beyond all worlds, until its spacious might
Satiate the void circumference: then shrink
Even to a point within our day and night;
And keep thy heart light, let it make thee sink
When hope has kindled hope, and lured thee to the brink.

Or go to Rome, which is the sepulchre,
Oh, not of him, but of our joy: 'tis nought
That ages, empires, and religions there
Lie buried in the ravage they have wrought;
For such as he can lend,—they borrow not
Glory from those who made the world their prey;
And he is gathered to the kings of thought
Who waged contention with their time's decay,
And of the past are all that cannot pass away.

Go thou to Rome,—at once the Paradise,
The grave, the city, and the wilderness;
And where its wrecks like shattered mountains rise,
And flowering weeds and fragrant corpses dress
The bones of Desolation's nakedness,
Pass, till the Spirit of the spot shall lead
Thy footsteps to a slope of green access,
Where, like an infant's smile, over the dead
A light of laughing flowers along the grass is spread;

And grey walls moulder round, on which dull Time
Feeds, like slow fire upon a hoary brand;
And one keen pyramid with wedge sublime,
Pavilioning the dust of him who planned
This refuge for his memory, doth stand
Like flame transformed to marble; and beneath,
A field is spread, on which a newer band
Have pitched in Heaven's smile their camp of death,
Welcoming him we lose with scarce extinguished breath.

Here pause: these graves are all too young as yet
To have outgrown the sorrow which consigned
Its charge to each; and if the seal is set,
Here, on one fountain of a mourning mind,
Break if not thou! too surely shalt thou find
Thine own well full, if thou returnest home,
Of tears and gall. From the world's bitter wind
Seek shelter in the shadow of the tomb.
What Adonais is, why fear we to become?

Yet again the thought of Death as the deliverer, the revealer, and the mystagogue, through whom the soul of man is reunited to the spirit of the universe, returns; and on this solemn note the poem closes. The symphony of exultation which had greeted the passage of Adonais into the eternal world, is here subdued to a graver key, as befits the mood of one whom mystery and mourning still oppress on earth. Yet even in the somewhat less than jubilant conclusion we feel that highest of all Shelley's qualities—the liberation of incalculable energies, the emancipation and expansion of a force within the soul, victorious over circumstance, exhilarated and elevated by contact with such hopes as make a feebler spirit tremble:

> The One remains, the many change and pass;
> Heaven's light for ever shines, Earth's shadows fly;
> Life, like a dome of many-coloured glass,
> Stains the white radiance of Eternity,
> Until Death tramples it to fragments.—Die,
> If thou wouldst be with that which thou dost seek!
> Follow where all is fled!—Rome's azure sky,
> Flowers, ruins, statues, music, words, are weak
> The glory they transfuse with fitting truth to speak.
>
> Why linger, why turn back, why shrink, my Heart?
> Thy hopes are gone before: from all things here
> They have departed; thou shouldst now depart!
> A light is past from the revolving year,
> And man and woman; and what still is dear
> Attracts to crush, repels to make thee wither.
> The soft sky smiles, the low wind whispers near:
> 'Tis Adonais calls! oh, hasten thither!
> No more let Life divide what Death can join together.
>
> That light whose smile kindles the Universe,
> That beauty in which all things work and move,
> That benediction which the eclipsing curse
> Of birth can quench not, that sustaining Love
> Which through the web of being blindly wove
> By man and beast and earth and air and sea,
> Burns bright or dim, as each are mirrors of
> The fire for which all thirst, now beams on me,
> Consuming the last clouds of cold mortality.
>
> The breath whose might I have invoked in song
> Descends on me; my spirit's bark is driven
> Far from the shore, far from the trembling throng
> Whose sails were never to the tempest given.
> The massy earth and sphered skies are riven!
> I am borne darkly, fearfully afar;
> Whilst burning through the inmost veil of Heaven,
> The soul of Adonais, like a star,
> Beacons from the abode where the Eternal are.

It will be seen that, whatever Shelley may from time to time have said about the immortality of the soul, he was no materialist, and no believer in the extinction of the spiritual element by death. Yet he was too wise to dogmatize upon a problem which by its very nature admits of no solution in this world. "I hope," he said, "but my hopes are not unmixed with fear for what will befall this inestimable spirit when we appear to die." On another occasion he told Trelawny, "I am content to see no farther into futurity than Plato and Bacon. My mind is tranquil; I have no fears and some hopes. In our present gross material state our faculties are clouded; when Death removes our clay coverings, the mystery will be solved." How constantly the thought of death as the revealer was present to his mind, may be gathered from an incident related by Trelawny. They were bathing in the Arno, when Shelley, who could not swim, plunged into deep water, and "lay stretched out at the bottom like a conger eel, not making the least effort or struggle to save himself." Trelawny fished him out, and when he had taken breath he said: "I always find the bottom of the well, and they say Truth lies there. In another minute I should have found it, and you would have found an empty shell. Death is the veil which those who live call life; they sleep, and it is lifted." Yet being pressed by his friend, he refused to acknowledge a formal and precise belief in the imperishability of the human soul. "We know nothing; we have no evidence; we cannot express our inmost thoughts. They are incomprehensible even to ourselves." The clear insight into the conditions of the question conveyed by the last sentence is very characteristic of Shelley. It makes us regret the non-completion of his essay on a "Future Life", which would certainly have stated the problem with rare lucidity and candour, and would have illuminated the abyss of doubt with a sense of spiritual realities not often found in combination with wise suspension of judgment. What he clung to amid all perplexities was the absolute and indestructible existence of the universal as perceived by us in love, beauty, and delight. Though the destiny of the personal self be obscure, these things cannot fail. The conclusion of the "Sensitive Plant" might be cited as conveying the quintessence of his hope upon this most intangible of riddles.

> Whether the Sensitive Plant, or that
> Which within its boughs like a spirit sat,
> Ere its outward form had known decay,
> Now felt this change, I cannot say.
>
> I dare not guess; but in this life
> Of error, ignorance, and strife,
> Where nothing is, but all things seem,
> And we the shadows of the dream:
>
> It is a modest creed, and yet
> Pleasant, if one considers it,
> To own that death itself must be,

Like all the rest, a mockery.

That garden sweet, that lady fair,
And all sweet shapes and odours there,
In truth have never passed away:
'Tis we, 'tis ours, are changed; not they.

For love, and beauty, and delight,
There is no death nor change; their might
Exceeds our organs, which endure
No light, being themselves obscure.

But it is now time to return from this digression to the poem which suggested it, and which, more than any other, serves to illustrate its author's mood of feeling about the life beyond the grave. The last lines of "Adonais" might be read as a prophecy of his own death by drowning. The frequent recurrence of this thought in his poetry is, to say the least, singular. In "Alastor" we read:—

A restless impulse urged him to embark
And meet lone Death on the drear ocean's waste;
For well he knew that mighty Shadow loves
The slimy caverns of the populous deep.

The "Ode to Liberty" closes on the same note: —

As a far taper fades with fading night;
As a brief insect dies with dying day,
My song, its pinions disarrayed of might,
Drooped. O'er it closed the echoes far away
Of the great voice which did its flight sustain,
As waves which lately paved his watery way
Hiss round a drowner's head in their tempestuous play.

The "Stanzas written in Dejection, near Naples", echo the thought with a slight variation:—

Yet now despair itself is mild,
Even as the winds and waters are;
I could lie down like a tired child,
And weep away the life of care
Which I have borne, and yet must bear,—
Till death like sleep might steal on me,
And I might feel in the warm air
My cheek grow cold, and hear the sea

Breathe o'er my dying brain its last monotony.

Trelawny tells a story of his friend's life at Lerici, which further illustrates his preoccupation with the thought of death at sea. he took Mrs. Williams and her children out upon the bay in his little boat one afternoon, and starting suddenly from a deep reverie, into which he had fallen, exclaimed with a joyful and resolute voice, "Now let us together solve the great mystery!" Too much value must not be attached to what might have been a mere caprice of utterance. Yet the proposal not unreasonably frightened Mrs. Williams, for Shelley's friends were accustomed to expect the realisation of his wildest fancies. It may incidentally be mentioned that before the water finally claimed its victim, he had often been in peril of life upon his fatal element—during the first voyage to Ireland, while crossing the Channel with Mary in an open boat, again at Meillerie with Byron, and once at least with Williams.

A third composition of the year 1821 was inspired by the visit of Prince Mavrocordato to Pisa. He called on Shelley in April, showed him a copy of Prince Ipsilanti's proclamation, and announced that Greece was determined to strike a blow for freedom. The news aroused all Shelley's enthusiasm, and he began the lyrical drama of "Hellas", which he has described as "a sort of imitation of the 'Persae' of Aeschylus." We find him at work upon it in October; and it must have been finished by the end of that month, since the dedication bears the date of November 1st, 1821. Shelley did not set great store by it. "It was written," he says, "without much care, and in one of those few moments of enthusiasm which now seldom visit me, and which make me pay dear for their visits." The preface might, if space permitted, be cited as a specimen of his sound and weighty judgment upon one of the greatest political questions of this century. What he says about the debt of the modern world to ancient Hellas, is no less pregnant than his severe strictures upon the part played by Russia in dealing with Eastern questions. For the rest, the poem is distinguished by passages of great lyrical beauty, rising at times to the sublimest raptures, and closing on the half-pathetic cadence of that well-known Chorus, "The world's great age begins anew." Of dramatic interest it has but little; nor is the play, as finished, equal to the promise held forth by the superb fragment of its so-called Prologue. (Forman, 4 page 95.) This truly magnificent torso must, I think, have been the commencement of the drama as conceived upon a different and more colossal plan, which Shelley rejected for some unknown reason. It shows the influence not only of the Book of Job, but also of the Prologue in Heaven to Faust, upon his mind.

The lyric movement of the Chorus from "Hellas", which I propose to quote, marks the highest point of Shelley's rhythmical invention. As for the matter expressed in it, we must not forget that these stanzas are written for a Chorus of Greek captive women, whose creed does not prevent their feeling a regret for the "mightier forms of an older, austerer worship." Shelley's note reminds the reader, with characteristic caution and frankness, that "the popular notions of Christianity are represented in this Chorus as true in their relation to the worship they superseded, and that which in all probability they will supersede, without considering their merits in a relation more universal."

Worlds on worlds are rolling over
From creation to decay,
Like the bubbles on a river
Sparkling, bursting, borne away.
But they are still immortal
Who, through birth's orient portal,
And death's dark chasm hurrying to and fro,
Clothe their unceasing flight
In the brief dust and light
Gathered around their chariots as they go;
New shapes they still may weave,
New gods, new laws receive;
Bright or dim are they, as the robes they last
On Death's bare ribs had cast.

A power from the unknown God,
A Promethan conqueror came;
Like a triumphal path he trod
The thorns of death and shame.
A mortal shape to him
Was like the vapour dim
Which the orient planet animates with light.
Hell, Sin, and Slavery came,
Like bloodhounds mild and tame,
Nor preyed until their Lord had taken flight.
The moon of Mahomet
Arose, and it shall set:
While blazoned as on heaven's immortal noon
The cross leads generations on.

Swift as the radiant shapes of sleep
From one whose dreams are paradise,
Fly, when the fond wretch wakes to weep,
And day peers forth with her blank eyes;
So fleet, so faint, so fair,
The Powers of earth and air
Fled from the folding star of Bethlehem:
Apollo, Pan, and Love
And even Olympian Jove,
Grew weak, for killing Truth had glared on them.
Our hills, and seas, and streams,
Dispeopled of their dreams,

Their waters turned to blood, their dew to tears,
Wailed for the golden years.

In the autumn of this year Shelley paid Lord Byron a visit at Ravenna, where he made acquaintance with the Countess Guiccoli. It was then settled that Byron, who had formed the project of starting a journal to be called "The Liberal" in concert with Leigh Hunt, should himself settle in Pisa. Leigh Hunt was to join his brother poets in the same place. The prospect gave Shelley great pleasure, for he was sincerely attached to Hunt; and though he would not promise contributions to the journal, partly lest his name should bring discredit on it, and partly because he did not choose to appear before the world as a hanger-on of Byron's, he thoroughly approved of a plan which would be profitable to his friend by bringing him into close relation with the most famous poet of the age. (See the Letter to Leigh Hunt, Pisa, August 26, 1821.) That he was not without doubts as to Byron's working easily in harness with Leigh Hunt, may be seen in his correspondence; and how fully these doubts were destined to be confirmed, is only too well known.

At Ravenna he was tormented by the report of some more than usually infamous calumny. What it was, we do not know; but that it made profound impression on his mind, appears from a remarkable letter addressed to his wife on the 16th and 17th of August from Ravenna. In it he repeats his growing weariness, and his wish to escape from society to solitude; the weariness of a nature wounded and disappointed by commerce with the world, but neither soured nor driven to fury by cruel wrongs. It is noticeable at the same time that he clings to his present place of residence:—"our roots never struck so deeply as at Pisa, and the transplanted tree flourishes not." At Pisa he had found real rest and refreshment in the society of his two friends, the Williamses. Some of his saddest and most touching lyrics of this year are addressed to Jane—for so Mrs. Williams was called; and attentive students may perceive that the thought of Emilia was already blending by subtle transitions with the new thought of Jane. One poem, almost terrible in its intensity of melancholy, is hardly explicable on the supposition that Shelley was quite happy in his home. ("The Serpent is shut out from Paradise.") These words must be taken as implying no reflection either upon Mary's love for him, or upon his own power to bear the slighter troubles of domestic life. He was not a spoiled child of fortune, a weak egotist, or a querulous complainer. But he was always seeking and never finding the satisfaction of some deeper craving. In his own words, he had loved Antigone before he visited this earth: and no one woman could probably have made him happy, because he was for ever demanding more from love than it can give in the mixed circumstances of mortal life. Moreover, it must be remembered that his power of self-expression has bestowed permanent form on feelings which may have been but transitory; nor can we avoid the conclusion that, sincere as Shelley was, he, like all poets, made use of the emotion of the moment for purposes of art, converting an ephemeral mood into something typical and universal. This was almost certainly the case with "Epipsychidion."

So much at any rate had to be said upon this subject; for careful readers of Shelley's minor poems are forced to the conviction that during the last year of his life he often found relief from a wretchedness, which, however real, can hardly be defined, in the sympathy of this true-hearted woman. The affection he felt for Jane was beyond question pure and honourable. All the verses he addressed to her passed through her husband's hands without the slightest interruption to their intercourse; and Mrs. Shelley, who was not unpardonably jealous of her Ariel, continued to be Mrs. Williams's warm friend. A passage from Shelley's letter of June 18, 1822, expresses the plain prose of his relation to the Williamses:—"They are people who are very pleasing to me. But words are not the instruments of our intercourse. I like Jane more and more, and I find Williams the most amiable of companions. She has a taste for music, and an eloquence of form and motions that compensate in some degree for the lack of literary refinement."

Two lyrics of this period may here be introduced, partly for the sake of their intrinsic beauty, and partly because they illustrate the fecundity of Shelley's genius during the months of tranquil industry which he passed at Pisa. The first is an Invocation to Night:—

> Swiftly walk over the western wave,
> Spirit of Night!
> Out of the misty eastern cave,
> Where all the long and lone daylight,
> Thou wovest dreams of joy and fear,
> Which make thee terrible and dear,—
> Swift be thy flight!
>
> Wrap thy form in a mantle grey
> Star-inwrought!
> Blind with thine hair the eyes of day,
> Kiss her until she be wearied out.
> Then wander o'er city, and sea, and land,
> Touching all with thin opiate wand-
> Come, long-sought!
>
> When I arose and saw the dawn,
> I sighed for thee;
> When light rode high, and the dew was gone,
> And noon lay heavy on flower and tree,
> And the weary Day turned to his rest,
> Lingering like an unloved guest,
> I sighed for thee.
>
> Thy brother Death came, and cried,
> "Wouldst thou me?"

Thy sweet child Sleep, the filmy-eyed,
Murmured like a noon-tide bee,
"Shall I nestle near thy side?
Wouldst thou me?"—and I replied,
"No, not thee!"

Death will come when thou art dead,
Soon, too soon—
Sleep will come when thou art fled;
Of neither would I ask the boon
I ask of thee, beloved Night—
Swift be thine approaching flight,
Come soon, soon!

The second is an Epithalamium composed for a drama which his friend Williams was writing. Students of the poetic art will find it not uninteresting to compare the three versions of this Bridal Song, given by Mr. Forman. (Volume 4 page 89.) They prove that Shelley was no careless writer.

The golden gates of sleep unbar
Where strength and beauty, met together,
Kindle their image like a star
In a sea of glassy weather!

Night, with all thy stars look down—
Darkness, weep thy holiest dew!
Never smiled the inconstant moon
On a pair so true.
Let eyes not see their own delight;
Haste, swift Hour, and thy flight
Oft renew.

Fairies, sprites, and angels, keep her!
Holy stars, permit no wrong!
And return to wake the sleeper,
Dawn, ere it be long.
O joy! O fear! what will be done
In the absence of the sun!
Come along!

Lyrics like these, delicate in thought and exquisitely finished in form, were produced with a truly wonderful profusion in this season of his happiest fertility. A glance at the last section of Mr. Palgrave's "Golden Treasury" shows how large a place they occupy among the permanent jewels of our literature.

The month of January added a new and most important member to the little

Pisan circle. This was Captain Edward John Trelawny, to whom more than to any one else but Hogg and Mrs. Shelley, the students of the poet's life are indebted for details at once accurate and characteristic. Trelawny had lived a free life in all quarters of the globe, far away from literary cliques and the society of cities, in contact with the sternest realities of existence, which had developed his self-reliance and his physical qualities to the utmost. The impression, therefore, made on him by Shelley has to be gravely estimated by all who still incline to treat the poet as a pathological specimen of humanity. This true child of nature recognized in his new friend far more than in Byron the stuff of a real man. "To form a just idea of his poetry, you should have witnessed his daily life; his words and actions best illustrated his writings." "The cynic Byron acknowledged him to be the best and ablest man he had ever known. The truth was, Shelley loved everything better than himself." "I have seen Shelley and Byron in society, and the contrast was as marked as their characters. The former, not thinking of himself, was as much at ease in his own home, omitting no occasion of obliging those whom he came in contact with, readily conversing with all or any who addressed him, irrespective of age or rank, dress or address." "All who heard him felt the charm of his simple, earnest manner: while Byron knew him to be exempt from the egotism, pedantry, coxcombry, and more than all the rivalry of authorship." "Shelley's mental activity was infectious; he kept your brain in constant action." "He was always in earnest." "He never laid aside his book and magic mantle; he waved his wand, and Byron, after a faint show of defiance, stood mute.... Shelley's earnestness and just criticism held him captive." These sentences, and many others, prove that Trelawny, himself somewhat of a cynic, cruelly exposing false pretensions, and detesting affectation in any for, paid unreserved homage to the heroic qualities this "dreamy bard,"—"uncommonly awkward," as he also called him—bad rider and poor seaman as he was—"over-sensitive," and "eternally brooding on his own thoughts," who "had seen no more of the waking-day than a girl at a boarding-school." True to himself, gentle, tender, with the courage of a lion, "frank and outspoken, like a well-conditioned boy, well-bred and considerate for others, because he was totally devoid of selfishness and vanity," Shelley seemed to this unprejudiced companion of his last few months that very rare product for which Diogenes searched in vain—a man.

Their first meeting must be told in Trelawny's own words—words no less certain of immortality than the fame of him they celebrate. "The Williamses received me in their earnest, cordial manner; we had a great deal to communicate to each other, and were in loud and animated conversation, when I was rather put out by observing in the passage near the open door, opposite to where I sat, a pair of glittering eyes steadily fixed on mine; it was too dark to make out whom they belonged to. With the acuteness of a woman, Mrs. Williams's eyes followed the direction of mine, and going to the doorway she laughingly said, 'Come in, Shelley, its only our friend Tre just arrived.' Swiftly gliding in, blushing like a girl, a tall, thin stripling held out both his hands; and although I could hardly believe, as I looked at his flushed, feminine, and artless face, that it could be the poet, I returned his warm pressure. After the ordinary greetings and courtesies he sat down and listened. I was silent from astonishment: was it possible this mild-looking, beardless boy, could be the veritable monster at war with all the world?—excommunicated by the Fathers of the Church, deprived of his civil rights by the fiat of a grim Lord Chancellor, discarded by every member of his family, and denounced by the rival sages of our literature as the founder of a Satanic school? I could not believe it; it must be a hoax. He was habited like a boy, in a black jacket and trousers, which he seemed to have outgrown, or his tailor, as is the custom, had most shamefully stinted him in his 'sizings.' Mrs. Williams saw my embarrassment, and to relieve me asked Shelley what book he had in his hand? His face brightened, and he answered briskly,-

"'Calderon's "Magico Prodigioso"—I am translating some passages in it.'

"'Oh, read it to us.'

"Shoved off from the shore of commonplace incidents that could not interest him, and fairly launched on a theme that did, he instantly became oblivious of everything but the book in his hand. The masterly manner in which he analysed the genius of the author, his lucid interpretation of the story, and the ease with which he translated into our language the most subtle and imaginative passages of the Spanish poet, were marvellous, as was his command of the two languages. After this touch of his quality I no longer doubted his identity; a dead silence ensued; looking up, I asked,—

"'Where is he?'

"Mrs. Williams said, 'Who? Shelley? Oh, he comes and goes like a spirit, no one knows when or where.'"

Two little incidents which happened in the winter of 1821-2 deserve to be recorded. News reached the Pisan circle early in December that a man who had insulted the Host at Lucca was sentenced to be burned. Shelley proposed that the English—himself, Byron, Medwin, and their friend Mr. Taafe—should immediately arm and ride off to rescue him. The scheme took Byron's fancy; but they agreed to try less Quixotic measures before they had recourse to force, and their excitement was calmed by hearing that the man's sentence had been commuted to the galleys. The other affair brought them less agreeably into contact with the Tuscan police. The party were riding home one afternoon in March, when a mounted dragoon came rushing by, breaking their ranks and nearly unhorsing Mr. Taafe. Byron and Shelley rode after him to remonstrate; but the man struck Shelley from his saddle with a sabre blow. The English then pursued him into Pisa, making such a clatter that one of Byron's servants issued with a pitchfork from the Casa Lanfranchi, and wounded the fellow somewhat seriously, under the impression that it was necessary to defend his master. Shelley called the whole matter "a trifling piece of business;" but it was strictly investigated by the authorities; and though the dragoon was found to have been in the wrong, Byron had to retire for a season to Leghorn. Another consequence was the exile of Count Gamba and his father from Tuscany, which led to Byron's final departure from Pisa.

The even current of Shelley's life was not often broken by such adventures. Trelawny gives the following account of how he passed his days: he "was up at six or seven, reading Plato, Sophocles, or Spinoza, with the accompaniment of a hunch of dry bread; then he joined Williams in a sail on the Arno, in a flat-bottomed skiff, book in hand, and from thence he went to the pine-forest, or some out-of-the-way place. When the birds went to roost he returned home, and talked and read until midnight." The great wood of stone pines on the Pisan Maremma was his favourite study. Trelawny tells us how he found him there alone one day, and in what state was the manuscript of that prettiest lyric, "Ariel, to Miranda take". "It was a frightful scrawl; words smeared out with his finger, and one upon the other, over and over in tiers, and all run together in most 'admired disorder;' it might have been taken for a sketch of a marsh overgrown with bulrushes, and the blots for wild ducks; such a dashed-off daub as self-conceited artists mistake for a manifestation of genius. On my observing this to him, he answered, 'When my brain gets heated with thought, it soon boils, and throws off images and words faster than I can skim them off. In the morning, when cooled down, out of the rude sketch as you justly call it, I shall attempt a drawing."

A daily visit to Byron diversified existence. Byron talked more sensibly with Shelley than with his commonplace acquaintances; and when he began to gossip, Shelley retired into his own thoughts. Then they would go pistol-shooting, Byron's trembling hand contrasting with his friend's firmness. They had invented a "little language" for this sport: firing was called tiring; hitting, colping; missing, mancating, etc. It was in fact a kind of pigeon Italian. Shelley acquired two nick-names in the circle of his Pisan friends, both highly descriptive. He was Ariel and the Snake. The latter suited him because of his noiseless gliding movement, bright eyes, and ethereal diet. It was first given to him by Byron during a reading of "Faust". When he came to the line of Mephistopheles, "Wie meine Muhme, die beruhmte Schlange," and translated it, "My aunt, the renowned Snake," Byron cried, "Then you are her nephew." Shelley by no means resented the epithet. Indeed he alludes to it in his letters, and in a poem already referred to above.

Soon after Trelawny's arrival the party turned their thoughts to nautical affairs. Shelley had already done a good deal of boating with Williams on the Arno and the Serchio, and had on one occasion nearly lost his life by the capsizing of their tiny craft. They now determined to build a larger yacht for excursions on the sea; while Byron, liking the project of a summer residence upon the Bay of Spezia, made up his mind to have one too. Shelley's was to be an open boat carrying sail, Byron's a large decked schooner. The construction of both was entrusted to a Genoese builder, under the direction of Trelawny's friend, Captain Roberts. Such was the birth of the ill-fated "Don Juan", which cost the lives of Shelley and Willliams, and of the "Bolivar", which carried Byron off to Genoa before he finally set sail for Greece. Captain Roberts was allowed to have his own way about the latter; but Shelley and Williams had set their hearts upon a model for their little yacht, which did not suit the Captain's notions of sea-worthiness. Williams overruled his objections, and the "Don Juan" was built according to his cherished fancy. "When it was finished," says Trelawny, "it took two tons of iron ballast to bring her down to her bearings, and then she was very crank in a breeze, though not deficient in beam. She was fast, strongly built, and Torbay rigged." She was christened by Lord Byron, not wholly with Shelley's approval; and one young English sailor, Charles Vivian, in addition to Williams and Shelley, formed her crew. "It was great fun," says Trelawny, "to witness Williams teaching the poet how to steer, and other points of seamanship. As usual, Shelley had a book in hand, saying he could read and steer at the same time, as one was mental, the other mechanical." "The boy was quick and handy, and used to boats. Williams was not as deficient as I anticipated, but over-anxious, and wanted practice, which alone makes a man prompt in emergency. Shelley was intent on catching images from the ever-changing sea and sky; he heeded not the boat."

CHAPTER 7

LAST DAYS

THE advance of spring made the climate of Pisa too hot for comfort; and early in April Trelawny and Williams rode off to find a suitable lodging for themselves and the Shelleys on the Gulf of Spezia. They pitched upon a house called the Villa Magni, between Lerici and San Terenzio, which "looked more like a boat or a bathing-house than a place to live in. it consisted of a terrace or ground-floor unpaved, and used for storing boat-gear and fishing-tackle, and of a single storey over it, divided into a hall or saloon and four small rooms, which had once been white-washed; there was one chimney for cooking. This place we thought the Shelleys might put up with for the summer. The only good thing about it was a verandah facing the sea, and almost over it." When it came to be inhabited, the central hall was used for the living and eating room of the whole party. The Shelleys occupied two rooms facing each other; the Williamses had one of the remaining chambers, and Trelawny another. Access to these smaller apartments could only be got through the saloon; and this circumstance once gave rise to a ludicrous incident, when Shelley, having lost his clothes out bathing, had to cross, in puris naturalibus, not undetected, though covered in his retreat by the clever Italian handmaiden, through a luncheon party assembled in the dining-room. The horror of the ladies at the poet's unexpected apparition and his innocent self-defence are well described by Trelawny. Life in the villa was of the simplest description. To get food was no easy matter; and the style of the furniture may be guessed by Trelawny's laconic remark that the sea was his only washing-basin.

They arrived at Villa Magni on the 26th of April, and began a course of life which was not interrupted till the final catastrophe of July 8. These few weeks were in many respects the happiest of Shelley's life. We seem to discern in his last letter of importance, recently edited by Mr. Garnett, that he was now conscious of having reached a platform from which he could survey his past achievement, and whence he would probably have risen to a loftier altitude, by a calmer and more equable exercise of powers which had been ripening during the last three years of life in Italy. Meanwhile, "I am content," he writes, "if the heaven above me is calm for the passing moment." And this tranquillity was perfect, with none of the oppressive sense of coming danger, which distinguishes the calm before a storm. He was far away from the distractions of the world he hated, in a scene of indescribable beauty, among a population little removed from the state of savages, who enjoyed the primitive pleasures of a race at one with nature, and toiled with hardy perseverance on the element he loved so well. His company was thoroughly congenial and well mixed. He spent his days in excursions on the water with Williams, or in solitary musings in his cranky little skiff, floating upon the shallows in shore, or putting out to sea and waiting for the landward breeze to bring him home. The evenings were passed upon the terrace, listening to Jane's guitar, conversing with Trelawny, or reading his favourite poets aloud to the assembled party.

In this delightful solitude, this round of simple occupations, this uninterrupted communion with nature, Shelley's enthusiasms and inspirations revived with their old strength. He began a poem, which, if we may judge of its scale by the fragment we possess, would have been one of the longest, as it certainly is one of the loftiest of his masterpieces. The "Triumph of Life" is composed in no strain of compliment to the powers of this world, which quell untameable spirits, and enslave the noblest by the operation of blind passions and inordinate ambitions. It is rather a pageant of the spirit dragged in chains, led captive to the world, the flesh and the devil. The sonorous march and sultry splendour of the terza rima stanzas, bearing on their tide of song those multitudes of forms, processionally grand, yet misty with the dust of their own tramplings, and half-shrouded in a lurid robe of light, affect the imagination so powerfully that we are fain to abandon criticism and acknowledge only the daemonic fascinations of this solemn mystery. Some have compared the "Triumph of Life" to a Panathenaic pomp: others have found in it a reflex of the burning summer heat, and blazing sea, and onward undulations of interminable waves, which were the cradle of its maker as he wrote. The imagery of Dante plays a part, and Dante has controlled the structure. The genius of the Revolution passes by: Napoleon is there, and Rousseau serves for guide. The great of all ages are arraigned, and the spirit of the world is brought before us, while its heroes pass, unveil their faces for a moment, and are swallowed in the throng that has no ending. But how Shelley meant to solve the problems he has raised, by what sublime philosophy he purposed to resolve the discords of this revelation more soul-shattering than Daniel's "Mene", we cannot even guess. The poem, as we have it, breaks abruptly with these words: "Then what is Life? I cried"—a sentence of the profoundest import, when we remember that the questioner was now about to seek its answer in the halls of Death.

To separate any single passage from a poem which owes so much of its splendour to the continuity of music and the succession of visionary images, does it cruel wrong. Yet this must be attempted; for Shelley is the only English poet who has successfully handled that most difficult of metres, terza rima. His power over complicated versification cannot be appreciated except by duly noticing the method he employed in treating a structure alien, perhaps, to the genius of our literature, and even in Italian used with perfect mastery by none but Dante. To select the introduction and part of the first paragraph will inflict less violence upon the "Triumph of Life" as a whole, than to detach one of its episodes.

> Swift as a spirit hastening to his task
> Of glory and of good, the Sun sprang forth
> Rejoicing in his splendour, and the mask
>
> Of darkness fell from the awakened Earth.
> The smokeless altars of the mountain snows

Flamed above crimson clouds, and at the birth

Of light, the Ocean's orison arose,
To which the birds tempered their matin lay.
All flowers in field or forest which unclose

Their trembling eyelids to the kiss of day,
Swinging their censers in the element,
With orient incense lit by the new ray,

Burned slow and inconsumably, and sent
Their odorous sighs up to the smiling air;
And, in succession due, did continent,

Isle, ocean, and all things that in them wear
The form and character of mortal mould,
Rise as the Sun their father rose, to bear

Their portion of the toil, which he of old
Took as his own, and then imposed on them.
But I, whom thoughts which must remain untold

Had kept as wakeful as the stars that gem
The cone of night, now they were laid asleep,
Stretched my faint limbs beneath the hoary stem

Which an old chestnut flung athwart the steep
Of a green Apennine. Before me fled
The night; behind me rose the day; the deep

Was at my feet, and Heaven above my head,—
When a strange trance over my fancy grew
Which was not slumber, for the shade it spread

Was so transparent that the scene came through
As clear as, when a veil of light is drawn
O'er evening hills, they glimmer; and I knew

That I had felt the freshness of that dawn
Bathe in the same cold dew my brow and hair,
And sate as thus upon that slope of lawn

Under the self-same bough, and heard as there
The birds, the fountains, and the ocean, hold
Sweet talk in music through the enamoured air.

And then a vision on my brain was rolled.

Such is the exordium of the poem. It will be noticed that at this point one series of the interwoven triplets is concluded. The "Triumph of Life" itself begins with a new series of rhymes, describing the vision for which preparation has been made in the preceding prelude. It is not without perplexity that an ear unaccustomed to the windings of the terza rima, feels its way among them. Entangled and impeded by the labyrinthine sounds, the reader might be compared to one who, swimming in his dreams, is carried down the course of a swift river clogged with clinging and retarding water-weeds. He moves; but not without labour: yet after a while the very obstacles add fascination to his movement.

As in that trance of wondrous thought I lay,
    This was the tenour of my waking dream:—
    Methought I sate beside a public way

Thick strewn with summer dust, and a great stream
    Of people there was hurrying to and fro,
    Numerous as gnats upon the evening gleam,

All hastening onward, yet none seemed to know
    Whither he went, or whence he came, or why
    He made one of the multitude, and so

Was borne amid the crowd, as through the sky
    One of the million leaves of summer's bier;
    Old age and youth, manhood and infancy,

Mixed in one mighty torrent did appear:
    Some flying from the thing they feared, and some
    Seeking the object of another's fear;

And others, as with steps towards the tomb,
    Pored on the trodden worms that crawled beneath,
    And others mournfully within the gloom

Of their own shadow walked and called it death;
    And some fled from it as it were a ghost,
    Half fainting in the affliction of vain breath.

But more, with motions which each other crossed,
    Pursued or spurned the shadows the clouds threw,
    Or birds within the noon-day ether lost,

Upon that path where flowers never grew—
And weary with vain toil and faint for thirst,
Heard not the fountains, whose melodious dew

Out of their mossy cells for ever burst;
Nor felt the breeze which from the forest told
Of grassy paths, and wood-lawn interspersed,

With over-arching elms, and caverns cold,
And violet banks where sweet dreams brood;—but they
Pursued their serious folly as of old.

Here let us break the chain of rhymes that are unbroken in the text, to notice the extraordinary skill with which the rhythm has been woven in one paragraph, suggesting by recurrences of sound the passing of a multitude, which is presented at the same time to the eye of fancy by accumulated images. The next eleven triplets introduce the presiding genius of the pageant. Students of Petrarch's "Trionfi" will not fail to note what Shelley owes to that poet, and how he has transmuted the definite imagery of mediaeval symbolism into something metaphysical and mystic.

And as I gazed, methought that in the way
The throng grew wilder, as the woods of June
When the south wind shakes the extinguished day;

And a cold glare, intenser than the noon
But icy cold, obscured with blinding light
The sun, as he the stars. Like the young moon—

When on the sunlit limits of the night
Her white shell trembles amid crimson air,
And whilst the sleeping tempest gathers might,—

Doth, as the herald of its coming, bear
The ghost of its dead mother, whose dim form
Bends in dark ether from her infant's chair;

So came a chariot on the silent storm
Of its own rushing splendour, and a Shape
So sate within, as one whom years deform,

Beneath a dusky hood and double cape,
Crouching within the shadow of a tomb.
And o'er what seemed the head a cloud-like crape

Was bent, a dun and faint ethereal gloom
Tempering the light. Upon the chariot beam
A Janus-visaged Shadow did assume

The guidance of that wonder-winged team;
The shapes which drew it in thick lightnings
Were lost:—I heard alone on the air's soft stream

The music of their ever-moving wings.
All the four faces of that charioteer
Had their eyes banded; little profit brings

Speed in the van and blindness in the rear,
Nor then avail the beams that quench the sun,
Or that with banded eyes could pierce the sphere

Of all that is, has been, or will be done.
So ill was the car guided—but it past
With solemn speed majestically on.

The intense stirring of his imagination implied by this supreme poetic effort, the solitude of the Villa Magni, and the elemental fervour of Italian heat to which he recklessly exposed himself, contributed to make Shelley more than usually nervous. His somnambulism returned, and he saw visions. On one occasion he thought that the dead Allegra rose from the sea, and clapped her hands, and laughed, and beckoned to him. On another he roused the whole house at night by his screams, and remained terror-frozen in the trance produced by an appalling vision. This mood he communicated, in some measure, to his friends. One of them saw what she afterwards believed to have been his phantom, and another dreamed that he was dead. They talked much of death, and it is noticeable that the last words written to him by Jane were these:—"Are you going to join your friend Plato?"

The Leigh Hunts arrived at last in Genoa, whence they again sailed for Leghorn. Shelley heard the news upon the 20th of June. He immediately prepared to join them; and on the 1st of July set off with Williams in the "Don Juan" for Leghorn, where he rushed into the arms of his old friend. Leigh Hunt, in his autobiography, writes, "I will not dwell upon the moment." From Leghorn he drove with the Hunts to Pisa, and established them in the ground-floor of Byron's Palazzo Lanfranchi, as comfortably as was consistent with his lordship's variable moods. The negotiations which had preceded Hunt's visit to Italy, raised forebodings in Shelley's mind as to the reception he would meet from Byron; nor were these destined to be unfulfilled. Trelawny tells us how irksome the poet found it to have "a man with a sick wife, and seven disorderly children," established in his palace. To Mrs. Hunt he was positively brutal; nor could he tolerate her self-complacent husband, who, while he had voyaged far and wide in literature, had never wholly cast the slough of Cockneyism. Hunt was himself hardly powerful enough to understand the true magnitude of Shelley, though he loved him; and the tender solicitude of the great, unselfish Shelley, for the smaller, harmlessly conceited Hunt, is pathetic. They spent a pleasant day or two together, Shelley showing the Campo Santo and other sights of Pisa to his English friend. Hunt thought him somewhat less hopeful than he used to be, but improved in health and strength and spirits. One little touch relating to their last conversation, deserves to be recorded:—"He assented warmly to an opinion I expressed in the cathedral at Pisa, while the organ was playing, that a truly divine religion might yet be established, if charity were really made the principle of it, instead of faith."

On the night following that day of rest, Shelley took a postchaise for Leghorn; and early in the afternoon of the next day he set sail, with Williams, on his return voyage to Lerici. The sailor-boy, Charles Vivian, was their only companion. Trelawny, who was detained on board the "Bolivar", in the Leghorn harbour, watched them start. The weather for some time had been unusually hot and dry. "Processions of priests and religiosi have been for several days past praying for rain;" so runs the last entry in Williams's diary; "but the gods are either angry or nature too powerful." Trelawny's Genoese mate observed, as the "Don Juan" stood out to sea, that they ought to have started at three a.m. instead of twelve hours later; adding "the devil is brewing mischief." Then a sea-fog withdrew the "Don Juan" from their sight. It was an oppressively sultry afternoon. Trelawny went down into his cabin, and slept; but was soon roused by the noise of the ships' crews in the harbour making all ready for a gale. In a short time the tempest was upon them, with wind, rain, and thunder. It did not last more than twenty minutes; and at its end Trelawny looked out anxiously for Shelley's boat. She was nowhere to be seen, and nothing could be heard of her. In fact, though Trelawny could not then be absolutely sure of the catastrophe, she had sunk, struck in all probability by the prow of a felucca, but whether by accident or with the intention of running her down is still uncertain.

On the morning of the third day after the storm, Trelawny rode to Pisa, and communicated his fears to Hunt. "I then went upstairs to Byron. When I told him, his lip quivered, and his voice faltered as he questioned me." Couriers were despatched to search the sea-coast, and to bring the "Bolivar" from Leghorn. Trelawny rode in person toward Via Reggio, and there found a punt, a water-keg, and some bottles, which had been in Shelley's boat. A week passed, Trelawny patrolling the shore with the coast-guardsmen, but hearing of no new discovery, until at last two bodies were cast upon the sand. One found near the Via Reggio, on the 18th of July, was Shelley's. It had his jacket, "with the volume of Aeschylus in one pocket, and Keats's poems in the other, doubled back, as if the reader, in the act of reading, had hastily thrust it away." The other, found near the tower of Migliarino, at about four miles' distance, was that of Williams. The sailor-boy, Charles Vivian, though cast up on the same day, the 18th of July, near Massa, was not heard of by Trelawny till the 29th.

Nothing now remained but to tell the whole dreadful truth to the two widowed women, who had spent the last days in an agony of alternate despair and hope at Villa Magni. This duty Trelawny discharged faithfully and firmly. "The next day I prevailed on them," he says, "to return with me to Pisa. The misery of that night and the journey of the next day, and of many days and nights that followed, I can neither describe nor forget." It was decided that Shelley should be buried at Rome, near his friend Keats and his son William, and that Williams's remains should be taken to England. But first the bodies had to be burned; and for permission to do this Trelawny, who all through had taken the lead, applied to the English Embassy at Florence. After some difficulty it was granted.

What remains to be said concerning the cremation of Shelley's body on the 6th of August, must be told in Trelawny's own words. Williams, it may be stated, had been burned on the preceding day.

"Three white wands had been stuck in the sand to mark the poet's grave, but as they were at some distance from each other, we had to cut a trench thirty yards in length, in the line of the sticks, to ascertain the exact spot, and it was nearly an hour before we came upon the grave.

"In the meantime Byron and Leigh Hunt arrived in the carriage, attended by soldiers, and the Health Officer, as before. The lonely and grand scenery that surrounded us, so exactly harmonized with Shelley's genius, that I could imagine his spirit soaring over us. The sea, with the islands of Gorgona, Capraja, and Elba, was before us; old battlemented watch-towers stretched along the coast, backed by the marble-crested Apennines glistening in the sun, picturesque from their diversified outlines, and not a human dwelling was in sight.

"As I thought of the delight Shelley felt in such scenes of loneliness and grandeur whilst living, I felt we were no better than a herd of wolves or a pack of wild dogs, in tearing out his battered and naked body from the pure yellow sand that lay so lightly over it, to drag him back to the light of day; but the dead have no voice, nor had I power to check the sacrilege—the work went on silently in the deep and unresisting sand, not a word was spoken, for the Italians have a touch of sentiment, and their feelings are easily excited into sympathy. Byron was silent and thoughtful. We were startled and drawn together by a dull, hollow sound that followed the blow of a mattock; the iron had struck a skull, and the body was soon uncovered.... After the fire was well kindled we repeated the ceremony of the previous day; and more wine was poured over Shelley's dead body than he had consumed during his life. This with the oil and salt made the yellow flames glisten and quiver. The heat from the sun and fire was so intense that the atmosphere was tremulous and wavy.... The fire was so fierce as to produce a white heat on the iron, and to reduce its contents to grey ashes. The only portions that were not consumed were some fragments of bones, the jaw, and the skull; but what surprised us all was that the heart remained entire. In snatching this relic from the fiery furnace, my hand was severely burnt; and had any one seen me do the act, I should have been put into quarantine."

Shelley's heart was given to Hunt, who subsequently, not without reluctance and unseemly dispute, resigned it to Mrs. Shelley. It is now at Boscombe. His ashes were carried by Trelawny to Rome and buried in the Protestant cemetery, so touchingly described by him in his letter to Peacock, and afterwards so sublimely in "Adonais". The epitaph, composed by Hunt, ran thus: "Percy Bysshe Shelley, Cor Cordium, Natus iv. August MDCCXCII. Obiit VIII Jul. MDCCCXXII." To the Latin words Trelawny, faithfullest and most devoted of friends, added three lines from Ariel's song, much loved in life by Shelley:

> Nothing of him that doth fade,
> But doth suffer a sea-change
> Into something rich and strange.

"And so," writes Lady Shelley, "the sea and the earth closed over one who was great as a poet, and still greater as a philanthropist; and of whom it may be said, that his wild spiritual character seems to have prepared him for being thus snatched from life under circumstances of mingled terror and beauty, while his powers were yet in their spring freshness, and age had not come to render the ethereal body decrepit, or to wither the heart which could not be consumed by fire."

CHAPTER 8

EPILOGUE

AFTER some deliberation I decided to give this little work on Shelley the narrative rather than the essay form, impelled thereto by one commanding reason. Shelley's life and his poetry are indissolubly connected. He acted what he thought and felt, with a directness rare among his brethren of the poet's craft; while his verse, with the exception of "The Cenci", expressed little but the animating thoughts and aspirations of his life. That life, moreover, was "a miracle of thirty years," so crowded with striking incident and varied experience that, as he said himself, he had already lived longer than his father, and ought to be reckoned with the men of ninety. Through all vicissitudes he preserved his youth inviolate, and died, like one whom the gods love, or like a hero of Hellenic story, young, despite grey hairs and suffering. His life has, therefore, to be told, in order that his life-work may be rightly valued: for, great as that was, he, the man, was somehow greater; and noble as it truly is, the memory of him is nobler.

To the world he presented the rare spectacle of a man passionate for truth, and unreservedly obedient to the right as he discerned it. The anomaly which made his practical career a failure, lay just here. The right he followed was too often the antithesis of ordinary morality: in his desire to cast away the false and grasp the true, he overshot the mark of prudence. The blending in him of a pure and earnest purpose with moral and social theories that could not but have proved pernicious to mankind at large, produced at times an almost grotesque mixture in his actions no less than in his verse. We cannot, therefore, wonder that society, while he lived, felt the necessity of asserting itself against him. But now that he has passed into the company of the great dead, and time has softened down the asperities of popular judgment, we are able to learn the real lesson of his life and writings. That is not to be sought in any of his doctrines, but rather in his fearless bearing, his resolute loyalty to an unselfish and in the simplest sense benevolent ideal. It is this which constitutes his supreme importance for us English at the present time. Ours is an age in which ideals are rare, and we belong to a race in which men who follow them so single-heartedly are not common.

As a poet, Shelley contributed a new quality to English literature—a quality of ideality, freedom, and spiritual audacity, which severe critics of other nations think we lack. Byron's daring is in a different region: his elemental worldliness and pungent satire do not liberate our energies, or cheer us with new hopes and splendid vistas. Wordsworth, the very antithesis to Shelley in his reverent accord with institutions, suits our meditative mood, sustains us with a sound philosophy, and braces us by healthy contact with the Nature he so dearly loved. But in Wordsworth there is none of Shelley's magnetism. $What remains of permanent value in Coleridge's poetry—such work as "Christabel", the "Ancient Mariner", or "Kubla Khan"—is a product of pure artistic fancy, tempered by the author's mysticism. Keats, true and sacred poet as he was, loved Nature with a somewhat sensuous devotion. She was for him a mistress rather than a Diotima; nor did he share the prophetic fire which burns in Shelley's verse, quite apart from the direct enunciation of his favourite tenets. In none of Shelley's greatest contemporaries was the lyrical faculty so paramount; and whether we consider his minor songs, his odes, or his more complicated choral dramas, we acknowledge that he was the loftiest and the most spontaneous singer of our language. In range of power he was also conspicuous above the rest. Not only did he write the best lyrics, but the best tragedy, the best translations, and the best familiar poems of his century. As a satirist and humourist, I cannot place him so high as some of his admirers do; and the purely polemical portions of his poems, those in which he puts forth his antagonism to tyrants and religions and custom in all its myriad forms, seem to me to degenerate at intervals into poor rhetoric.

While his genius was so varied and its flight so unapproached in swiftness, it would be vain to deny that Shelley, as an artist, had faults from which the men with whom I have compared him were more free. The most prominent of these are haste, incoherence, verbal carelessness, incompleteness, a want of narrative force, and a weak hold on objective realities. Even his warmest admirers, if they are sincere critics, will concede that his verse, taken altogether, is marked by inequality. In his eager self-abandonment to inspiration, he produced much that is unsatisfying simply because it is not ripe. There was no defect of power in him, but a defect of patience; and the final word to be pronounced in estimating the larger bulk of his poetry is the word immature. Not only was the poet young; but the fruit of his young mind had been plucked before it had been duly mellowed by reflection. Again, he did not care enough for common things to present them with artistic fulness. He was intolerant of detail, and thus failed to model with the roundness that we find in Goethe's work. He flew at the grand, the spacious, the sublime; and did not always succeed in realizing for his readers what he had imagined. A certain want of faith in his own powers, fostered by the extraordinary discouragement under which he had to write, prevented him from finishing what he began, or from giving that ultimate form of perfection to his longer works which we admire in shorter pieces like the "Ode to the West Wind". When a poem was ready, he had it hastily printed, and passed on to fresh creative efforts. If anything occurred to interrupt his energy, he flung the sketch aside. Some of these defects, if we may use this word at all to indicate our sense that Shelley might by care have been made equal to his highest self, were in a great measure the correlative of his chief quality—the ideality, of which I have already spoken. He composed with all his faculties, mental, emotional, and physical, at the utmost strain, at a white heat of intense fervour, striving to attain one object, the truest and most passionate investiture for the thoughts which had inflamed his ever-quick imagination. The result is that his finest work has more the stamp of something natural and elemental—the wind, the sea, the depth of air—than of a mere artistic product. Plato would have said: the Muses filled this man with sacred madness, and, when he wrote, he was no longer in his own control. There was, moreover, ever-present in his nature an effort, an aspiration after a better than the best this world can show, which prompted him to blend the choicest products of his thought and fancy with the fairest images borrowed from the earth on which he lived. He never willingly composed except under the impulse to body forth a vision of the love and light and life which was the spirit of the power he worshipped. This persistent upward striving, this earnestness, this passionate intensity, this piety of soul and purity of inspiration, give a quite unique spirituality to his poems. But it cannot be expected that the colder perfections of Academic art should always be found in them. They have something of the waywardness and negligence of nature, something of the asymmetreia we admire in the earlier creations of Greek architecture. That Shelley, acute critic and profound student as he was, could conform himself to rule and show himself an artist in the stricter sense, is, however, abundantly proved by "The Cenci" and by "Adonais". The reason why he did not always observe this method will be understood by those who have studied his "Defence of Poetry", and learned to sympathize with his impassioned theory of art.

Working on this small scale, it is difficult to do barest justice to Shelley's life or poetry. The materials for the former are almost overwhelmingly copious and strangely discordant. Those who ought to meet in love over his grave, have spent their time in quarrelling about him, and baffling the most eager seeker for the truth. (See Lady Shelley v. Hogg; Trelawny v. the Shelley family; Peacock v. Lady Shelley; Garnett v. Peacock; Garnett v. Trelawny; McCarthy v. Hogg, etc., etc.) Through the turbid atmosphere of their recriminations it is impossible to discern the whole personality of the man. By careful comparison and refined manipulation of the biographical treasures at our disposal, a fair portrait of Shelley might still be set before the reader with the accuracy of a finished picture. That labour of exquisite art and of devoted love still remains to be accomplished, though in the meantime Mr. W.M. Rossetti's Memoir is a most valuable instalment. Shelley in his lifetime bound those who knew him with a chain of loyal affection, impressing observers so essentially different as Hogg, Byron, Peacock, Leigh Hunt, Trelawny, Medwin, Williams, with the conviction that he was the gentlest, purest, bravest, and most spiritual being they had ever met. The same conviction is forced upon his biographer. During his four last years this most loveable of men was becoming gradually riper, wiser, truer to his highest instincts. The imperfections of his youth were being rapidly absorbed. His self-knowledge was expanding, his character mellowing, and his genius growing daily stronger. Without losing the fire that burned in him, he had been lessoned by experience into tempering its fervour; and when he reached the age of twenty-nine, he stood upon the height of his most glorious achievement, ready to unfold his wings for a yet sublimer flight. At that moment, when life at last seemed about to offer him rest, unimpeded activity, and happiness, death robbed the world of his maturity. Posterity has but the product of his cruder years, the assurance that he had already outlived them into something nobler, and the tragedy of his untimely end.

If a final word were needed to utter the unutterable sense of waste excited in us by Shelley's premature absorption into the mystery of the unknown, we might find it in the last lines of his own "Alastor":—

> Art and eloquence,
> And all the shows o' the world, are frail and vain
> To weep a loss that turns their light to shade.
> It is a woe "too deep for tears," when all
> Is reft at once, when some surpassing spirit,
> Whose light adorned the world around it, leaves
> Those who remain behind nor sobs nor groans,
> The passionate tumult of a clinging hope;
> But pale despair and cold tranquillity,
> Nature's vast frame, the web of human things,
> Birth and the grave, that are not as they were.

THE END.

Printed in the United Kingdom
by Lightning Source UK Ltd.
133959UK00002B/177/A

9 781406 808995